Sit down and stay for a while. We know you'll want seconds. Besides, life always tastes better when shared!

(Kora and Lloyd Hollinger, serving it up right in the early 1970s in the dining room of their home in Russell, Kansas)

DEDICATION

This book is lovingly dedicated to the amazing Kora Marie (Lindenmeyer) Hollinger, who has been an incredible inspiration, a wealth of knowledge, a vessel of endless humor, and a dedicated Grandmother. I began this journey seven years ago with the idea that I would write her life story and present it to her on her 100th birthday. Well, as we all know, life has a habit of getting in the way of things. One year turned into two which eventually turned into seven years.

At one point during this process, Grandma jokingly directed me, "Just get the dang book written so I can go!" I suppose I figured that the longer it took me to write it, the longer she'd be with us. Perseverance is an understatement when it comes to this woman!

Thanks for rocking it all of these years, Grandma!

I also dedicate this book to the memory of my grandpa, Lloyd "Sal" Hollinger. It's been over 30 years since you left us, but your spirit still resides within us. Grandma misses you every single day....and then some!

Finally, if only my dad, L.A. Hollinger, M.D. could be here to see this come to fruition. His premature departure from this world in 1993 was not an easy experience for us, but I know he continues to look down upon us from Heaven, most likely smiling upon Grandma, wondering what she's going to be up to next.

ACKNOWLEDGEMENTS

There are so many individuals whom I want to thank for their support, input, guidance, and encouragement on this book. If I have failed to recognize anyone in any way, please know that you will always be remembered in my heart for the contributions you made. Without the help and support of the following people, this book would never have come to fruition:

Kora Hollinger
Susan Hollinger
Steve Hollinger
Mr. and Mrs. William H. Told, Jr.
Blaine Hollinger
Judy Hollinger
Kitty Hollinger
Jeff Hollinger
Laurie Hollinger
Cindy Hollinger Cassity
Walter Cassity
Jed Keys
Senator Robert J. Dole
The late Wendall Anschutz
Catherine Holland
Joyce Gorton
Norma Jean Cook
Stratton Lindenmeyer
Brian Dumler

And the many townspeople of Russell, Kansas, and other friends and family of Kora who gave of their time to provide special insight, tid bits, and stories that have given flavor to this book

A special thank you goes to the following colleagues:

David "Big Bob" Elyachar
Harry G. Baum, Ed.D.
Dan Bolen, Chairman of the Bank of Prairie Village
www.empowher.com

And, finally, a special nod to my husband Ed and our three boys, Alec, Zach, and Noah, for putting up with me as I tirelessly worked to complete this book. It wasn't always easy, but it was worth the endeavor!

Koraspondence: Living Life to the Letter

By Ann Hollinger Butenas

Copyright ©2011 Ann Hollinger Butenas

Published by MeritCare Health Systems, Inc.

Printed by Proforma Marketing & Promotional Solutions

For additional information, please contact the author at: ann@korashouse.com

Front and back cover design by:

Karen Tapp, tappdance design, llc

Edited by: Lisa Allen, *www.backtoallen.com*

Printed in the United States

Koraspondence: Living Life to the Letter

ISBN 10: 0983450218

ISBN 13: 978-0-9834502-1-4

KORA MARIE LINDENMEYER HOLLINGER
BORN FEBRUARY 22, 1905

INTRODUCTION

I started to write this book in 2004, as my grandmother was approaching her 100th birthday. However, with life throwing various punches at me during that time, I never really got past Chapter One. Now, over six years later, with my grandma still gracing our lives with her energetic presence, I decided that her story had to be written.

I want to write not only about what she has experienced over the past century, but how a life well-lived such as hers can work as an inspiration and guiding light for those of us who desire to achieve only a mere portion of what she has achieved.

Kora Marie Lindenmeyer (Hollinger is her married name), born on February 22, 1905, is more than just a human on this Earth. She is a spiritual presence to those who know her. She is equal parts inspiring and enigmatic. She combines wit, fervor, and personal opinions with an unparalleled grace. To those of us who personally know her, she is a sort of icon....a legend, perhaps, yet just as physically human as the rest of us. As former Senate Majority Leader and US Presidential candidate, Bob Dole, once told me, "Kora is always on full throttle!"

Grandma has maintained a personal steadfastness in her life that continues to propel her as she climbs to a physical age that many of us might never realize. As I begin to write this book, I have to question the universal forces that have persuaded me to bring this book to light: "Is Grandma still among us so that I may capture her life in a manner to which others can relate and from which they can be inspired?" Or, is she merely hanging around so that one day, she may benefit from my will? I prefer to think it is the former. She will joke it is the latter.

To that end, I have decided to share with you not just a life story, but an illustration of how we can achieve more than we thought possible; how we can live our lives in a manner that somewhat selfishly sees the importance in ourselves, yet takes that confidence, embraced by genuine compassion, and spills it into the lives of those with whom we come in contact.

I hope that you enjoy reading this book. May it elicit an abundance of emotions, from tears to laughter to eventual self-reflection. After all, as the song by Five for Fighting relates, "You only have 100 years to live." May you all realize more than a century of a life well-lived! Grandma most assuredly gives living testament to the notion that even if you are approaching the evening of your life, that doesn't mean the sun has to go down anytime soon!

A BRIEF HISTORY OF KORA MARIE LINDENMEYER HOLLINGER

My grandmother, Kora Marie Lindenmeyer, was born on February 22, 1905 in Dorrance, Kansas. She was one of six children of Minnie and Henry Lindenmeyer. Her siblings included two brothers, Fred and Clarence, and two sisters, Sadie and Carolyn. A third brother, Franklin, died when he was just six days old. Grandma is eternally grateful for the love and support that were continually provided to her by her parents over the years.

"They were the nicest parents for which I could have ever asked," she noted.

In 1908, Grandma and her family moved to Russell, Kansas. By 1921, she graduated from high school in what she describes as a stunning feat.

"I completed high school in just three years," she proudly beamed.

Grandma then attended Washburn University in Topeka, Kansas with an academic emphasis on music. Once her collegiate days were behind her, she returned to her home in Russell. Less than a year later, a cute young fellow by the name of Lloyd Hollinger, also of Russell and four years her senior, asked her out on a date. She accepted, and the rest is history. My grandparents walked down the aisle to wedded bliss on March 28, 1927. Together, they had two sons, L.A. and Blaine, both of whom attended the University of Kansas for undergraduate degrees and for medical school.

Not one to let academics fall to the wayside for herself, Grandma also attended business school in Salina, Kansas and pursued a career in secretarial work for a host of local oil companies and attorneys in her home town.

When L.A. and Blaine were grown and out of the nest, this gave my grandparents ample time to do things together. Raising two ambitious and active boys all those years, as well as operating a thriving business - Hollinger Drug – for 40 years together, the two celebrated their 50th wedding anniversary in 1977 with a host of family and friends joining in on the festivities with them.

Just two years later, Lloyd died suddenly from an aneurysm in the heart. Although I had witnessed Grandma crying from time to time over the years, the tears she shed when her "Lloydie" died were more like waterfalls. He was the light of her life. However, as a woman with true inner strength, she still continued on with her life, not one to let the burdens of life weigh her down. Her stumbling blocks have always become stepping stones.

Heartache struck once again for Grandma in 1993, as she watched her oldest son, my dad, L.A., pass away from complications due to an 18-month-long struggle with brain cancer. He was just a few weeks shy of his 60th birthday and just a few months shy of walking me down the aisle to be married.

Despite the ups and downs of her life, Grandma has lived a rich existence on a host of levels. Her travels have taken her to many foreign countries including Russia, Egypt, Panama, Alaska, France, Hawaii, and Germany. She is a huge University of Kansas fan (she says Kansas State is okay, but they're second to the Jayhawks. Don't even get her started on the University of Missouri, though! Dangerous territory!).

Grandma fancies herself a "bridge maniac" and could play the game for hours. She has earned several bridge trophies over the years. And if you presume to play with her, you'd better be at the top of your game...or even better!

Grandma has always maintained close ties with her family. When Grandma's children were babies, her mother lived next door. Grandma would wave a diaper out the window as a signal that she needed help and her mother would come to help with the children, diapering or feeding or tending to whatever was needed. To the best of my knowledge, that was the first Instant Message!

Grandma has taken the whole family on a number of vacations, most recently on a cruise to Mexico in July 2010 (while she covered the expense for 22 people in all, only 20 could be in attendance.). This was Grandma's 29th cruise.

Referring to her six grandchildren and nine great-grandchildren, she says "They're all smart kids." What the family has always gotten a kick out of is the way Grandma will forlornly say at the conclusion of each adventure, "This may be my last trip with all of you. I'm getting old, you know." We heard this comment repeatedly throughout the 1970s, 1980s, 1990s, and into the 21st century. Still do. However, at the end of our most recent cruise, Grandma pulled me aside and enthusiastically whispered into my ear, "Let's do this again in five years." (Do the math. She was 105 when she said that! Optimism at its finest!)

The Hollingers always led a deeply religious life. They attended Otterbein United Methodist Church in Russell, where Grandma played the piano and the organ for 75 years until she retired at the age of 95, without ever taking a single paycheck for her contributions! The family dog Snoopy "worked" at the drug store and often accompanied the family to church. When they were out of town, Snoopy still went to church when he heard the bells ringing. To add to this distinction, Grandma holds the record for being the longest continuous member of Otterbein United Methodist Church in Russell, Kansas at 96 years and counting. She was just 10 years old when she joined.

Grandma is a very generous person. She has a history of doing nice things for others, including donating a new organ to Otterbein Church, and often paying for the Otterbein youth group to go on their ski trips. She helped a young couple, Tony and Luchi Racela, from the Philippines whom Blaine brought to the U.S. in the 1960s after he completed a fellowship in that country. The Racelas didn't have anything when they arrived in the United States, and my grandparents helped them get started by giving them housewares, furniture, and other items essential to starting a home. The Racelas eventually enjoyed successful careers as doctors in Kansas City, raising two amazing daughters, and are now enjoying retirement.

Grandma talks about playing bridge with Bob Dole's mother, and visiting Bob in the hospital after he returned from the war with several injuries. While the townspeople were pampering Bob, Grandma told him to "get up and quit lying around."

So, what exactly is the secret to Grandma's longevity? It's basically one simple habit that has sustained her: "You just keep going and exercising. I've exercised all my life; I don't mean running every day, but just staying active." As to how she produced such successful sons, Grandma will just smile and wink, "Because they had a successful mother."

So, sit back, relax, and enjoy a journey of faith, love, hope, peace, and laughter as you learn a few things about Grandma and her amazing life. It is intended to be less autobiographical and more inspirational. Take from it what you will. I don't expect folks to agree with everything, nor do I expect Grandma to be seen as a saint. She is who she is, and that is what makes this book special.

(Thanks to Joyce Gorton and the Russell County News for their assistance in compiling this information through an interview with Grandma in April 2010.)

GRANDMA, AGE 5, AND HER YOUNGER BROTHER CLARENCE, AGE 3, CHILLING ON THE FRONT PORCH OF THEIR HOME IN RUSSELL, KANSAS, CIRCA 1910.

THE LEAST YOU SHOULD KNOW ABOUT GRANDMA KORA

→ World traveler

→ Unofficial world record holder – over 70 years as church organist at the same church

→ Mom to two sons, both born on the same day – two years apart, both leading scholars, both became medical doctors

→ Owned a pharmacy in Russell, Kansas, with her husband that not only survived, but thrived, during the Great Depression, largely due in part to their efforts in sharing in their rewards with their community

→ Never met a buffet she didn't like

→ Has always enjoyed new dining experiences and has been known to pick dining places from Triple A ratings, dining on top of the Mark in San Francisco and in the Space Needle when the World's Fair was held in Seattle

→ Grandmother to six

→ Great-grandmother to nine

→ Role model to all

→ True to one – herself

→ Will always speak her mind and enjoy the results

→ Eats salt like candy. "I'm well preserved!" she will joke.

→ Loves Kansas University football and basketball – big Jayhawks fan – and once told legendary basketball great, Wilt Chamberlin, who played on the same college team with her youngest son, that he had a foul mouth and should watch his language!

GRANDMA KORA, AT AGE 103, AND HER GRANDSON, JEFF
HOLLINGER, TAKING THE SCENIC ROUTE ON A COLORADO
ADVENTURE...SUMMER 2008. "LET THE GOOD TIMES ROLL
AND ENJOY THE RIDE! BOY, HOWDY!" AS GRANDMA WOULD
SAY!

WHAT DOES "KORASPONDENCE" MEAN?

When I refer to correspondence, I don't just mean communication delivered through letters. Over the past century and then some, Grandma has communicated with me, as well as with countless others, through every form of communication possible...telegrams, phone calls, hand-written letters, face-to-face encounters, facial expressions, body language, shouts across the room or in the stadium, through e-mail, and even through the technological power of Skype. Grandma has never been afraid to speak her mind and enjoy the results. The power of correspondence to her meant getting your word across and having your voice heard...and then respectfully listening to the responses in return. You have to remain confident in yourself, but you must also respect the values, ideas, and opinions of others, even if you don't always agree with them.

Correspondence to me now means always maintaining an open line of communication with those who mean the most to you in life. While Grandma has harbored few regrets in her life, she has always told me that she wished she had openly expressed to her family over the years how much she loved them. Sure, she knew they knew, but she just wished she had expressed it more.

Now, at 106 years of age, she will admit that life can sometimes get lonely.

"Not only have your friends died, but their kids have died, and even the kids of their kids are getting on in years," she has reflected. "Always remember to keep in touch with family, no matter what. Friends come and go. Family is there to stay."

And she didn't just mean the immediate family, either. Numerous times she has reminded me to keep in touch with my cousins, my aunts, my uncles, etc.

"You don't want to realize the significant impact they had on your life after they've gone," she said. "Let them know now. Go to Heaven knowing you did that."

I had to ask her, upon hearing that message, "Is that why you think God has kept you here on Earth? Do you have some unfinished business?"

Without missing a beat, and true to her unflappable sense of humor, Grandma then laughed, "I think Heaven is just too crowded right now. They need to kick some of the dumb ones out, I suppose. I mean...where do they keep all of those people? They have to be running out of room by now." She's never been one to wax philosophical for too long.

She momentarily paused and cast a quizzical eye to the skies. Perhaps in her mind's eye, she sees a "No Vacancy" sign in the sky. That's fine by me. I don't mind having her down here at all, as long as she is healthy and happy.

So...she waits....and continues her mission to inspire us all. She doesn't have to tell us she loves us. We've known that all along.

As you journey through life, remember to keep the lines of communication continually open with those you love. Make regular "Koraspondence" a way of life. Reconnect with those with whom you have lost touch. Make a connection with a stranger and hopefully that will evolve into friendship. Your "Koraspondence" throughout life will be your continuing legacy. Make every word count.

(And for the record, Grandma made efficient use of her time when she wrote letters to friends and family.

She would frequently begin each letter with the words, "Dear One and All," and would proceed to draft the body of the letter. She would then make several copies of the letter and mail it out to everyone! That way, she just had to write or type one letter, while sending it to dozens of people simultaneously! That wasn't e-mail....it was K-mail! Reply all!)

As you can see, Grandma makes good use of every square inch on her hand-written postcards to us. The only challenge is in reading it! How a woman of her age even at that time could write in such small letters just baffles me! However, it was important to her to get her entire message across to the recipient, and she has always been a stickler for details in a letter! She endeavored to get her stamp's worth on the card!

Nov 79

Dear L.A. and Susan,

Guess I'll dash off a few lines before going up-stairs this morning--it's about 8 o'clock. I've taken my exercises and when I finish with this, I'll dress and go down and get the mail. Nothing press in this morning. Go to club this P.M. and choir practice tonight.

How was the week end with Steve home? And did he arrive back in Tulsa okay? I mailed him a check yesterday for $16. for those tickets. Why did you let him send this to me? You heard me tell him, that no matter what he sold them for, it was his to keep. I'm proud of him for selling them for as much as he did.

Boy, I was really lonesome Friday P.M. and night and just couldn't shake it. Was so glad when it was time to go to bed, knowing I would go to sleep and awaken to another day, but Sat. wasn't much better. Did go out to the Ramada Inn in morn with Loretta and Ivan for coffee. In P.M. watched the OU-NU game, boy it was good and later in P.M. the Cunninghams came over for a while and in the evening we 3 went out to eat a bite. Sunday I was okay. In the eve Celeste and I went out for a sandwich. Am enclosing my check for $30 for the nuts, which I forgot to give you. Celeste paid me her $15.00.

Put the trash out yesterday morn--that was a job, some tubs I had to pull out there. Was afraid they wouldn't take it all and I was out there when they put it in, and told them I was sorry I had so much, etc. but they took it all but the tires and asked if I cared if they could wait and take them the next time, which is Friday. Faith had told me she was almost sure they wouldn't take tires, but they took the rug and everything. So that was great. Garage looks great, and I do so appreciate you L.A. and Steve doing this. I wrote Steve yesterday. I found the adder--thought someone had taken it--but

Limestone posts, with a pioneer personality, have supported their barbed wire fences around thousands of prairie acres in North Central Kansas since the 1870's. Still standing guard, they reflect the sturdy character of the pioneers whose ingenuity conceived and erected them on their almost treeless homesteads. No two posts are quite alike in size, shape, or the natural color that time and nature has weathered on their surfaces. This post-rock area is marked by the use of stone posts, from the western border of Washington County southwest for almost two hundred miles into northern Ford County. In width the fencepost area ranges from ten to forty miles. The counties included in this area are Republic, Jewell, Osborne, Mitchell, Cloud, Ottawa, Lincoln, Russell, Rooks, Ellis, Ness, Rush, Barton, Ellsworth, Pawnee, and Hodgeman. It is estimated that about forty thousand miles of post-rock fence can be traced throughout this area. The first use of the limestone was for building rock. It was uncovered from outcroppings, "sledged" out by hand and dressed with stone hammers. Because of its availability and abundance, it was soon extensively used for construction of homes, schools, churches, bridges, posts, decorative stone, and other structural purposes. Soon a method of quarrying was used where holes were drilled into the limestone strata about eight inches apart. Feathers and wedges were placed in the holes and the wedges lightly pounded until the rock split in desired widths. Water was sometimes poured in the holes in the winter and the expansion of the freezing water would split the stone. The era of quarrying rock for fence posts has been practically over since the 1920's. Increased prices of stone posts compared to wooden and steel posts caused their quarrying to be generally discontinued. These two-toned light tan, rusty-brown stone posts with weathered dark irregular patches dress the prairie landscape with a distinctiveness not found elsewhere.

Steve must have put it away. I looked all over the yard and in the garage and it bothered me if someone had come inside the yard and taken it--but later found it behind the door as you go in to the garage, so when you entered and opened the door it was concealed. Some gal came one day and asked if she could have the bicycle wheels so she took them.

You know L.A. I thought my taxes were only what was on that one sheet, $590. but all told I paid $836. Isn't that ridiculously high for me? I paid it yesterday. Also, by now, am sure Wash had told you about their trip out here. I was sorry they wouldn't stay and let me buy their lunch, but know he wanted to get back. When he went in to Dick's office, they had all those papers ready for him, so appreciated that from Dick. Then got up to the courthouse an hour earlier than supposed to, but he took us too, and was very nice to Wash. I sent him a note of thanks.

Of course, since Sunday I've been busy anyway, so that helped. Mr. Holzer died and I kept Eleanor and Al's kids, 3 of them over night Sunday night and for breakfast Monday morn. So more bedding--to wash--the funeral was Monday P.M. which I played for.

Filled my car up since returning from game--filled it myself--some gal went with me to watch me do it--I did it tho. Unleaded 99.9 and I figured it out and averaged since going to the game and what driving I've done since going to that game, 15 plus to the gal. Oh, yes, called Fred Sat. mornand his legs were hurting him so much he couldn't come and I really hated it then, since I was so lonesome and had so much food, but then later it worked out better, since I had those kids coming n Sunday to keep. Had the preacher and wife over last night for my last left-overs . How was your casserole? And when did you have it? I was over to the Cunninghams Monday night for dinner--she had the Haneys also and Maurine Ralph--Haneys left yesterday morn for Texas for the winter.

Still don't know what to do Xmas--I'm going to see a couple about going with me--I can't see driving alone and bet by now couldn't get plane to Houston and such trouble getting to Wichita and I looked at Braniff book and on some of their flights they take you in to K.C. and then to Houston. Isn't that silly? So might as well go to K.C. and take plane.

Well, nothing else--wish it would warm up so I could wash my car now. Thanks for coming out! Love

mother

Your envelope - plan to get me a sticker but haven't ordered them yet - will work great!

This is another testament to Grandma's letter writing prowess. As evidenced in this particular letter, she not only typed an appreciable amount, but she later added last minute thoughts in handwriting around the edges. Note the stationery, too! She always used stationery that she could pick up for free somewhere...from hotels, banks, restaurants....you name it! She has always been thrifty!

FIRST GRADE CLASS PHOTO, CIRCA 1910
GRANDMA IS ON THE FAR LEFT, SECOND ROW, IN WHITE.
SHOULD WE CONSIDER A CLASS REUNION IN THE NEAR
FUTURE?

APPRECIATE THE POWER OF A WARM CUP OF COFFEE!

Stuck in a torrential downpour one gloomy Saturday afternoon in the heart of Austin, Texas, Grandma and some of her family members, eager to have the skies clear up so they could head over to the University of Texas football stadium to indulge their passion for the game, were simply looking for a place to change out of their wet clothes and get cleaned up. All they really needed was the use of a hotel room for just a couple of hours. Grandma's youngest son, Blaine, pulled up to a nearby hotel and went inside to ask the clerk if he could pay for a room just for the afternoon. Returning to the car, he told his passengers, "They don't allow that sort of thing." Blaine's wife, Judy, then declared she could get them to agree to it, so in she went, full of purpose, only to return several minutes later with the same response. Unfazed, Grandma, in her 90s at the time, said, "Let me show you how it's done." She got out of the car and confidently marched into the hotel lobby. After several long minutes, she returned to the car with not one, but two, sets of hotel room keys. When asked how she managed to get the hotel clerk to do that, she replied, "Easy. I just appealed to his sense of kindness. I sat him down and engaged him over a cup of coffee, told him our predicament, and he was fine with it. What's the problem?"

BE AN ENTHUSIASTIC COACH!

Now that she lives in Houston, close to her son and his family, Grandma enjoys attending the basketball practices and games of a local girls' high school team one of her grandsons coaches. Even into her 100s, Grandma will sit patiently, yet very intently, on the sidelines, cheering on the girls and will then wisely advise them after the game or practice as to what techniques they should be working on. Simultaneously, she will praise them for a job well done.

When you encourage others, it makes you feel good, and when you feel good, you simply glow. You glow, Grandma!

IF EATING WAS AN OLYMPIC SPORT, GRANDMA WOULD TAKE HOME THE GOLD!

So...you think you know what the primary food groups are, huh? Sit down to dine with Grandma, and you will learn otherwise! Her main food groups include gravy, cream, sauces, salt, salt, and more salt.

She'd crack herself up many times at meal time by saying, "When I run out of butter, I'm going to grease!"

She always encouraged me to try a variety of foods.

"You don't have to like everything," she would stress. "Just give things a try, though. Don't be so particular. Folks don't like it when one is particular."

Grandma is pretty boastful about her appetite, too.

"I can eat anything, anytime, anywhere, under any circumstances, cooked any way, with anything," she has always emphasized.

However, she does caution those who are inclined to over-indulge:

"Eat well, but don't eat too much. Don't get fat. Maintain your figure. I've still got mine!"

What is interesting to note about Grandma is that in all of her travels around the world, from continent to continent, she will jokingly tell you that she may not be able to recall everything she saw in her travels, but she sure can tell you all about what she ate!

Her catch phrase at every meal? "Good eatin'!"

"WHAT'S THIS? YOU KNOW I'VE ALWAYS TOLD YOU, 'IF I CAN'T EAT IT, I DON'T WANT IT!'" GRANDMA GETTING HER CHRISTMAS GROOVE ON IN 1980.

AND SPEAKING OF FOOD...

Grandma and food go way back. She loves to eat. She loves to cook. She loves to entertain. Every adventure, every occasion, and every day is a celebration of food. While she is eating breakfast, she is planning the lunch menu. When preparing for upcoming vacations, her first order of business is to find out where to eat and when to eat. She has traveled the world, from Europe to Africa, from the Panama Canal to Russia. Forget about sight-seeing, although that was always on the agenda, but keep the focus on the local flavor! Grease and salt. Those are her two main food groups. Grandma lives on salt. Several years ago, when pondering what to get her for her birthday, several family members and I thought about chipping in and buying her a salt lick she could set up in the back yard and go to as her heart desired, much like a deer would. Give Grandma a shaker of salt, and she is good to go. Throw in some grease, and you have a real party going on! (And if you own a restaurant in which Grandma is dining, hide the salt shakers and sugar packets, as well as those little jelly packs. One year, after collecting those for quite some time, she made a hodge-podge jelly mix by opening up all of those little packs of jelly and mixing them together into empty fruit jars. Instant holiday gifts for friends and loved ones!)

Doctors of today would have a fit with her diet. In fact, it would downright make them cringe. However, Grandma has remained perfectly healthy and has never even had issues with weight, cholesterol, or blood pressure. Grease and salt run freely through her veins. I firmly believe that is what keeps her alive. Yes, she is quintessentially well-preserved. She eats at McDonald's several times a week. (She likes the free coffee for seniors. She also likes those value breakfast meals!) To Grandma, McDonald's is 5-Star caliber! On her 100th birthday, her local McDonald's congratulated her with her official McDonald's jacket. I believe she would work there if she had the time, but she is just too busy!

Last year, Grandma did provide a subtle reference about her health, indicating she was contemplating "firing" her doctor. When I asked her why, her response seemed quite logical.

"He can't find a dang thing wrong with me, and at my age, you'd think an experienced doctor could find something wrong with me," she laughed.

ALWAYS IN IT FOR A GOOD LAUGH, GRANDMA PRETENDS TO HANG ON FOR DEAR LIFE OVER A GENTLY FLOWING STREAM IN THE COLORADO ROCKIES IN 1971.

THIS IS AS FAR BACK AS I CAN RECALL

My earliest memory of my grandma dates back to the mid-1960s when I was about two or three years of age. My older brother and I were spending a week with my grandparents at their modest home in Russell, Kansas, as we usually did each summer. I was going to sleep on an old roll-away bed in her musty basement which actually served as her "master bedroom."

Tucked safely in, I began to stick my thumb into its usual and comfortable spot in my mouth. Grandma, in all of her zest, came over to me, yanked the barely wet thumb from my mouth, and rubbed something on it that was supposed to make me not want to suck on it. However, in my shock from her actions, I accidentally poked my eye with the thumb and caused it to become inflamed. From what Grandma tells me, she began to get worried about my eye. It was better by morning, but I think it shook my rather unflappable granny up a bit. It never deterred her, however, from disciplining me more throughout the years. Even now, I still endure her endless counseling and scolding via the phone or in letters. However, from my oldest memories of her until now, there exists quite a bit of storytelling about Grandma. Some of it is quite fascinating. Some of it is humorous. Some of it may have you questioning her behavior. But most of it will leave you with a feeling of awe and wonder of how this woman, in her 107th year of life now, continues to carry on with such flamboyance and, well, attitude.

WHAT DO GRANDMA AND STEVEN SPIELBERG HAVE IN COMMON?

When Grandma came out to Los Angeles in 1987 to visit me, we spent that entire week shopping, going to the movies, chasing celebrities, and eating! It was an incredible week! Grandma had more energy than I did, and she was always scheming something exciting to do! However, she also knew that I still had to put my nose to the grindstone and find a good job.

Not one to mess around professionally, Grandma put her list of contacts and associates to work and managed to arrange an interview for me at CBS Television Studios in Studio City with Steve Mills, who was vice president of the network at that time. Mr. Mills was also a former resident of Russell, a town that seems to breed so many interesting, creative, and high-profile people. It must be something in the water. Even former Pennsylvania Senator Arlen Specter hails from that small Kansas town. I am convinced that Russell has a certain aura about it. And how about Marj Dusay? At one time this Russell gal dated Uncle Blaine. She is an actress best known for her role on the soap opera, "Guiding Light." (From what I have been told, she broke my uncle's heart, but that's another story for another day!)

As I was still very wet behind the ears in the entertainment industry, Grandma went with me to the interview. Now, by that I mean she rode along in the car with me and sat outside and snoozed while I conducted business with the big dogs behind studio gates.

"Don't embarrass me!" she yelled out the car window as I nervously went inside for my interview. I felt like a dumpy Midwestern girl in a glamorized world where everyone looked like royalty. I was like Cinderella without the glass slipper. This was never going to work out for me.

I managed to get through the hour-long process with Mr. Mills, who was very nice, yet painfully honest. While I probably did not have a future in front of the camera (my acting skills were horrendous!), he did seem intrigued by my writing skills. Even though he had no position available at the time, he implied that I might find employment in television and film from a creative standpoint.

I am sure he was really just doing a favor for Grandma, but it was exciting for me to be around such celebrity that day! In fact, that particular interview led me to another one just a few short weeks later with Richard Rosenbloom, then president of Orion Television. He granted me an hour of his time one sunny Tuesday afternoon in late 1987. Even then, I knew I was a fish out of water, but the thrill was still there for me! I was in Hollywood rubbing elbows with some pretty big names, and I had Grandma to thank for it!

That particular interview then led me to a meeting with Zev Braun, a well-known television and movie producer, and that ultimately led me to a meeting with one of Steven Spielberg's key people. However, I totally messed up that interview. Grandma was not in Los Angeles when I was scheduled for this one, which is probably why it went so poorly.

I was living in Westwood, which is a town contiguous to Beverly Hills. The interview with

Spielberg's people was over near Universal City, quite a distance away up the 405 and down the 101. Not wanting to be unsure of how to get there on the big day, I drove the route the night before the interview, so I would be certain of where I was going. I didn't want to look like an idiot...especially an idiot with Kansas license plates on her car. I received a lot of comments about that when I was out there! (No, I don't know Dorothy and I'm quite certain that I don't have a dog named Toto! And guess what? We have paved roads, too; not yellow bricks!)

Fate was not with me on the morning of the interview. You see, I drove that route around nine o'clock the night before. The interview was for nine in the morning the next day. In Los Angeles, at that time, there was a big difference in the amount of traffic at 9 p.m. versus 9 a.m. on those freeways. What took me roughly 30 minutes or so the night before stretched into well over two hours the next day. I was late and missed out on the opportunity, but I sure did meet some interesting folks on the freeway, er, parking lot!

During my time living near Hollywood, I managed to meet a lot of celebrities and have those once-in-a-lifetime experiences. However, if Grandma had moved out there and become my roommate, I am convinced that we would own that town by now!

"KORA! THIS IS GOD. GO TO THE LIGHT. I REPEAT. GO DIRECTLY TO THE LIGHT."

These powerful words vibrated in the deepest recesses of 105-year-old Kora Hollinger's ear (Yes...ear, not ears...more on this later. Be patient!) one evening in July 2010. However, they must have just hit a wall and bounced right back out, as Kora barely took notice of them, preferring instead to eat her dinner and get on with her evening. Some say God speaks to us in strange ways, but this probably had to be one of the most unique ways in which God attempted to make His presence known to this feisty woman whom he had been tracking for over a century.

When God speaks, though, that doesn't mean we will always listen, and in the case of my 105-year-old grandmother, if God doesn't communicate at just the right moment, He'll have to take a number (and preferably not hers!) and get in line. Kora has things to do and people to see. "I just don't have time to die," she has frequently said. Even if God makes His presence known on a Carnival cruise ship out in the middle of the ocean, that still might not be the right time to grab Kora's attention. True to her proverbial style, she had things to do. If God was going to interrupt her, it would have to be on her time, not His. This particular afternoon was no exception.

The weather outside could not have been more idyllic. The warm sun still cast its brilliant, late afternoon glow across the shiny blue seas. A few billowy clouds decorated the pure sky. Light winds brought about sweet-smelling ocean breezes, and the peaceful waves dancing across the ocean's surface were both mesmerizing and soothing.

Inside, the first dinner bell had just rung. Guests who had signed up for the early meal had already shuffled into their assigned seats in the main dining room. This eleven-year-old family cruise ship had only been at sea for two days, so the hungry travelers were still all-too eager to indulge their taste buds in the bountiful flavors that were soon to come. Hundreds of excited travelers filled the room. There were a few empty chairs, probably reserved for those who thought they had their sea legs, but were probably still in their cabins, warding off the evils of sea sickness.

Without missing a beat, Kora had already found her seat and had settled in. Her white, crisp linen napkin was spread across her lap. Her water glass, filled just minutes before, bore witness to her thirsty mouth as a faint lipstick stain embraced its outer rim. She reached for the bread basket and then for a pad of butter.

"Where's my dang knife?" she asked anyone within earshot. "I can't eat my bread without my butter."

The rest of her extended family, all 18 of them, were finding their seats and preparing for the delicious meal ahead. The dining room was a bustling affair of chattering patrons, busy servers, and noisy young kids who, despite just having filled themselves up with burgers and fries on the Lido Deck just two hours earlier, were already complaining of being "so hungry."

My uncle Blaine, age 75, had recently purchased a headset and microphone ensemble that Grandma could use so that she could enjoy all of the dialogue during the noisy meal with her family. Of all of her faculties in life, her sense of hearing has been the one most notably affected with time and age. When she was in her mid-70s, she awakened one morning and while walking around the kitchen, she felt a loud pop go off in her left ear. Initially startled, she soon realized that she was completely deaf in that ear. She could hear nothing. Nada. Zilch.

Relatively unfazed, Grandma did see a doctor about it later that day, and he merely confirmed what she already knew.

"Yes, Kora," he diagnosed. "You are deaf in that ear." Grandma must have shot him a look that suggested, "No kidding? I could have told you that. Now you expect me to pay you?"

So, we all learned over the years, if you have something good to say about Grandma, sit on her starboard side. If you have something negative to say, position yourself on her port side.

The headset Grandma was using during this adventure was actually kind of bulky, similar to what radio talk show hosts and DJs might wear while on the air. There was a little black receiver box with a small dial that could be adjusted so that Grandma could determine the volume of what she heard. The corded microphone plugged into the box, and the cord was long enough so that it could reach people across the table and down at the other end if they wanted to converse with Grandma without shouting at the top of their lungs. If she liked what you had to say, the dial was turned up. If she disagreed with you, the dial was turned down. If she felt you had nothing better to say, the headset just came off.

During this particular meal, words of a more thundering nature echoed within her ears. As our entire family was eating their dinner, my cousin Jeff decided to play a little trick on our grandmother. Unbeknownst to Grandma, Jeff had taken the microphone and had pulled it back to our table, which was just behind

Grandma's table. (With 19 of us in the group, we were divided amongst two dining tables.)

Grandma was sitting at her table with her back to us. Jeff and I were facing the same direction as Grandma at the other table, so we had a clear view of her backside and all of her activity. Jeff elbowed me in the ribs and said, "Watch this," as he put the microphone close to his mouth and slowly said the words in a deep, clear, and highly commanding voice: "Kora. This is God. Go to the light. Go to the light."

At first, it did not appear Grandma had heard this mandate. Jeff assured me he had turned up the volume on the box. Grandma was just too busy eating her meal. So, he firmly and confidently repeated his request: "Kora. I said this is God. Please go to the light. I have been waiting for you for a very long time. Go to the light."

By this time, I was cracking up so hard that I had almost wet my pants, something Jeff's sense of humor had always managed to make me do ever since we were little kids. After this second request from "God," we noticed that Grandma had temporarily put her fork down and lifted her head, looking left to right to see who could have possibly said that to her.

Jeff once again repeated into the microphone, "That's right. You heard me. This is God. Go to the light."

Grandma looked around once again. She did not utter a word. As the silence lingered and she apparently did not see any angels or hear any harps playing in the distance, she simply shrugged her shoulders and resumed eating. When there's food involved, Grandma doesn't have time to go to the light. God would just have to wait; her food was getting cold and she was running low on salt. That was truly an issue far more urgent and compelling than dealing with God.

KORASPONDENCE GOES HI-TECH: FROM THE PONY EXPRESS TO SKYPE!

While Grandma Kora was not around during the establishment of the Pony Express back in 1860, her primary mode of cross-country communication "back in the day" was more akin to that than of what we have surrounded ourselves with today. Over the past century, Grandma has been a consumer of the telegraph, the postage stamp, the telephone, and the quick shout across the back alley to contact a neighbor – the original instant message! She has witnessed the evolution of communication in ways this generation will never imagine. For Grandma, her experience with communication across the lines went high-tech as we celebrated her 106th birthday via Skype.

On Saturday, March 5, 2011, Grandma was kicking it up and rocking it out at her birthday celebration at the assisted living facility in Houston where she now lives. As I could not physically be there with her, due to time and monetary constraints, I asked my cousin Jeff if we could take advantage of Skype technology and give me the opportunity to participate that way.

We successfully arranged the lines of video communication shortly after the party began. Jeff "showed" me around the place and introduced me to the party-goers while carrying me around on his lap top! When Grandma had a break in conversation with other people, he put the computer in front of her. Initially, she seemed a bit confused, and even inquired of Jeff, "How did you get those people in the computer?" She simultaneously began to push different keys on the keyboard while Jeff warned me, "Ann, if she keeps this up, we may lose you!"

Grandma finally released her fingers from the keyboard and slowly came to the realization that we were having a video chat. For someone who by all accounts is more familiar with the workings of the Pony Express instead of express technology, this was just another rite of passage for Grandma. Up next? Holograms!

At any rate, I enjoyed chatting with Grandma via the computer. Of course, my three sons, my husband, and my mom were all in the room with me, so Grandma got to visit with the whole group. She would ramble on about her day, what she was eating, and then she held up her hands to show us her freshly-manicured nails. At 106, it is still important for Grandma to be presentable. Jeff even pulled the computer away from Grandma for a bit so we could see her outfit.

Even though we enjoyed each other's company for the thirty minutes or so we "Skyped" together that day, I still do miss those small little white postcards with a million words crammed onto them as Grandma conveyed to me every breath she took during her day. Don't misunderstand me. Technology is great, and it has its place, but the hand-written form of communication is a lost and dying art, and I wish that others would take up where Grandma left off and resurrect a tradition that creates memories and adds to the pages of our lives.

Don't Even THINK About Placing a Collect Call if Grandma Kora is on the Receiving End!

Going away to college was a pretty big deal for me. Although the campus I was attending was less than an hour away from home, I still fell victim to the inevitable freshman homesickness blues. In retrospect, it was probably less a matter of homesickness and more a matter of me not getting my way. You see, when I was a senior in high school, I was a rather ambitious soul. I still am, but in a different way. I was of the belief that you did not graduate from high school with merely a resume, but with a biography. I was involved in many activities in my high school – sports, clubs, band, theater – whatever I could join that would look good on a college application. Driven was an understatement. I also made sure to get straight "As" most of the time. To fall below giving 100% of my efforts to anything was just not acceptable to me.

When it came time for me to apply to college, the West Coast was all that was on my mind. I actually wanted to pursue a career in film-making. I had been a published writer since age 12 and knew that my creativity would eventually land my work on the big screen. As such, I made applications to a few schools in Southern California...as close to the "HOLLYWOOD" sign as I could get. I also applied up north to Stanford, just for good measure. I signed and dated the applications, put them in their respective envelopes, sealed them, and mailed them off, confident that my fate would arrive a month or so later in the form of an acceptance letter.

On the day that the mail man did deliver responses from the universities to which I applied, I was not disappointed. Even though I still had a semester of high school to complete, I was ready to pack my bags. After all, I contemplated; it is never too soon to begin your future. Little did I know that the brakes would be hit hard and my glorious ride would come to a screeching halt.

"What????" I am sure I screamed at my parents after they delivered their never-anticipated response to my acceptances. "I got accepted to these great schools, put on the waiting list for another, and you are telling me I can't go! That is so unfair!" I am sure I stomped around and made a big scene, much like any 17-year-old girl who could not get her way. However, this was a very big deal to me. This was my future. I knew what I wanted to do and the steps I thought I needed to take to get there. Putting a fence around the state of Kansas would seriously create a road block for me.

In my parents' eyes, those schools were just too far away, and the thought of their little girl going to school in such a big city did not make them feel very comfortable. No, they advised, I would be getting my education closer to home.

For them, "closer to home" was just an alternative way of saying, "You're going to the University of Kansas." From my perspective, however, my dream had just been buried....or at least put off for another four years. Despite their urging that I attend KU, their alma mater, I opted to apply to and take advantage of my acceptance to Baker University, a private Methodist school in Baldwin City, Kansas, located about 20 minutes away from the KU campus.

I knew KU was a great school, but I was being stubborn. I figured if I could not have my way, no one else could, either. I know...very silly, but from a 17-year-old hormonal girl's perspective, it was the obvious answer.

By the fall of 1981, I was packing my bags and gearing up for my collegiate career. I cannot say I was very enthusiastic about it all. I really did not know much about this school, other than the fact that my cousin had been there for a couple of years already and he loved it. There! That was my expert advice on the topic. To Baker I would go.

I settled into my dorm room, awkward, uncomfortable, and very frustrated that I was even doing this. However, I was not going to change my mind and go to KU. My first few weeks in college were miserable. I felt out of place, socially inept, and, in a word, miserable. I was not happy with my choice, but the only other option was KU, and I was not going to give in to that suggestion. I did stick it out for four years, eventually becoming very involved on campus. I wrote for the school newspaper, had a leadership role in my sorority, and played on the varsity tennis team for three years. Was it a bad experience? No. Was it the experience I desired? Not really. However, I did receive a good education, made some friends, and greatly improved my backhand swing in tennis. I even managed to complete the requirements for graduation in three and a half years. I simply stuck out my final semester to take some fun classes and play tennis. I figured that perhaps one day I could attend graduate school at the university of my choice. Interestingly enough, however, I ended up getting my Master's degree from Baker 11 years later with my husband shortly after we got married, an endeavor we chose to do together. Who knew?

At any rate, during my first semester at Baker, I called home frequently. Presumably, it was to touch base and let my parents know how I was doing. I perfected my tone of voice to suggest I was in hell and that I was completely miserable. Was I honestly that miserable? No, but in my heart, I really did not want to be there. I also used those frequent phone calls to encourage my parents to put a bit more money into the checking account. On one occasion, I made my routine call back home, collect, of course, as that's just the way things were done back in 1981. The phone rang several times with no answer, and as I was just about to hang up, a familiar voice picked up on the other end and said, "Y'ellow." In my family, whenever someone answered the phone saying "y'ellow," you knew it had to be Grandma Kora. For some reason, she had this way of making "hello" start with a "y." That always annoyed me for some reason. It was akin to referring to the wash as "warsh." Chills.

Before I could say a word, the operator interjected, "I have a collect call from Ann. Will you accept the charges?" As my parents had always agreed to the charges, what I wanted to say was on the tip of my tongue, ready to fall off at any moment, only to be sucked back in unexpectedly when Grandma said rather defiantly, "No, I will not accept the charges. Send a letter." Then, she hung up the phone.

Dumbfounded, appalled, and well, down-right insulted, I tried again. Same reply. I waited a few hours before I put myself through this punishment again, and was grateful to hear my mom's voice on the other end. She explained to me that my grandmother did not want to accept the charges for a collect call because she was worried that my parents would be upset with her if she did.

"What if I was dying or injured or my eye balls were falling out of their sockets?" I demanded to know. My mom sighed and just simply replied, "That's just Grandma."

After I settled down a bit, I began to understand the rationale behind Grandma's response. Communicating by letter was just her style. Phone calls, especially those that required long-distance charges, were for emergency use only. And for Grandma, an emergency meant that you were dead, dying, or late for dinner. After that one particular instance with the collect call, I often wondered if I had sent Grandma a letter bearing the words, "Postage Due," would she reject that, too? I've never had the courage to find out.

"C'MON! YOU NEED ANOTHER CUP OF COFFEE!"

Sometimes, a brief encounter with Grandma Kora can leave a person touched (or scarred, depending on your perspective! LOL!) for life. There is a certain essence about her that has literally remained dormant and untapped in so many others. Confidence is purely an understatement when it comes to this woman. She knows what she wants, when she wants it, and how she wants it....and no one better get in her way in the process.

A few years ago, I was hosting my weekly Saturday morning radio show, and I had a wonderful guest on the show named Jerry Smith who was enlightening the audience about his professional coaching business. I had only just met this man at a networking event, but was immediately charmed by his English accent. That accent alone would bring in more listeners, I thought, so on the air we went! In all seriousness, my radio show was about entrepreneurial business endeavors, so Jerry was a great fit.

As was customary during the show, I had a segment on the show reserved for "Conversations with Kora," in which I played pre-recorded interview bits with Grandma about any number of topics. At the bottom of the hour, I played that day's piece. Shortly thereafter, and much to my surprise, Jerry informed me, on air, that he had been in Grandma's kitchen once. Dead air is not a good thing in radio. Briefly surprised, I was left speechless. I then asked him something along the lines of "Are you sure?" After all, to the best of my knowledge, this man was from England. What did he know about a little old lady from a small town in Kansas, and further...what had he been doing in her kitchen, for crying out loud?

As Jerry began to explain his story, it dawned on me that he was married to a woman who, as a child, had spent some time with my grandparents in their hometown of Russell while her parents went off to a seminar for several days. Her parents, Tony and Luchi Racela, were the two people befriended by my grandparents years ago when the moved to the states from the Philippines, which is how the connection was then made.

At any rate, Jerry proceeded to convey an amusing, if not downright delightful, tale about his one and only encounter with Kora.

"We met up with her at McDonald's, and I believe it was on a Saturday morning," noted Jerry. "As I understood it, she had a rather large social circle, and McDonald's was the proverbial meeting place."

As Jerry, his wife, their kids, and the Drs. Racela enjoyed breakfast with Grandma, it was not long before the coffee pot ran dry and Grandma grew anxious. Coffee is her morning elixir....the hotter the better...and seeing as how McDonald's customarily does not employ waitresses, Grandma took it upon herself to take care of business.

As Jerry continued, "She literally got up – she's 103 years old now, mind you – and proceeded to the ordering counter. She did not just stop there, but she walked behind the counter, grabbed a pot of hot coffee and brought it back over to our table and commenced to freshen our cups. She's 103 years old and taking charge of the situation! I found that literally amazing."

Jerry also had the inspired opportunity to spend a bit of time with Grandma at her home, along with the rest of his family. It was not until I had a conversation with him later on that I suddenly had an accurate description of Grandma's home, which has been around since the beginning of the 20th century.

"When I went into her home," emphasized Jerry, "I had suddenly walked into a time capsule."

That's it! Her home is a time capsule! Amazingly true! Sure...it had always smelled musty and stale to me, and as a child, I just figured that's what old people smelled like, but Jerry opened my eyes to the fact that it was a literal museum of sorts, with items and memorabilia that have traveled a lifetime and then some. We may one day have to donate her home and all of its belongings to the Smithsonian. I can see it now...a "Kora's House" display....right next to George Washington's false teeth.

IT'S SUMMER TIME AND THE LIVING IS, WELL, INTERESTING...

What I remember most about spending time with my grandmother was when my older brother and I would head off to her home in Russell, Kansas, each summer for one week. This was a tradition established by my parents, most likely to give them a week's reprieve from my brother and me. After our week's stay at Grandma and Grandpa's home, my parents would drive west on I-70 from our home in suburban Kansas City to pick us up and take us for another two-week vacation in the Colorado Rockies.

That week we spent each summer with our grandparents was both exciting and frightening! I don't mean to sound as if my grandmother scared us, but let's just say she had an overbearing presence and a way of making sure we did things her way and her way only! My grandpa was the more relaxed and laid back of the two. He basically just went along with anything my grandma insisted on doing, as I don't really think he thought he had much of a choice in the matter anyway.

Whenever my grandmother would stress me out, I either found myself hiding out in her basement, or sitting upon my grandpa's lap while he grabbed one of my feet and serenaded me with his favorite song, "Put your little foot right there." I am not quite sure where he learned that song, or, for that matter, what it really meant, but it comforted me, and that is all that mattered at the time.

In her usual assertive style, Grandma had the whole week planned out for my brother and I, most of which was spent sitting in the presence of people whom, to me, appeared just as old, if not older, than my grandparents. Even though my grandparents were barely into their 70s at the time, they seemed pretty ancient to me. Now, with a grandma over the age of 100 and myself in my 40s, age 70 seems rather youthful!

We endured a host of picnics, swimming time at the Elks Club (Grandma was quite adamant that we hang on to the side of the pool and do 200 leg kicks with her each day! To Grandma, I attribute my healthy thighs!), dashes to McDonald's, and time in their corner drugstore, Hollinger Drug.

Hollinger Drug was a refuge from my grandparents' musty old home. While Grandpa, a pharmacist, carried out his apothecarial duties, I would explore the store and all of its contents. Grandpa would also make sodas and shakes for my brother and me at the old-fashioned soda counter. This was the kind of soda shoppe/pharmacy where you could find just about any type of chewed up gum stuck under the table tops. At the time, that actually grossed me out. Now, with one of those old tables in my mom's basement, I wonder from whom each of those pieces of gum came. Maybe each piece had a story to tell.

Church attendance was a huge requirement, as well! Grandma was the church organist, and she was ever-faithful in that capacity! We were required to sit in the front pew as an apparent means to keep us out of mischief during the service. Grandpa sang in the choir. I can still see Grandma turning her head and putting her finger to her mouth to "shush" us when we were chatting during the service. No doubt, we heard about THAT later! She also had a rearview mirror strategically placed on the organ so she could keep a keen eye on us the whole time.

Back in those days...those days being the 1970s....mail was delivered on Sundays in Russell, Kansas. So, after church, we would walk across the uneven brick street to the post office to see what was hiding in Box 271. Grandma and Grandpa knew everyone in their little town. As such, it took about twenty minutes to make that trek across the street, as they would stop and chat with everyone. Grandma would cheerfully introduce us to her friends and neighbors. We had to smile and act gracious. I just could not wait to get back to their house to get out of my itchy church clothes and into my shorts and t-shirt.

Other sources of entertainment during those week-long stays included sitting on one of the two divans in their front room while Grandma watched either her "stories" or any sports event. We had to remain absolutely silent during that time. Sometimes, it was extremely painful to sit there and endure programming that had no interest whatsoever to me.

I would soon find myself outdoors in the bright sunshine taking a bike ride about town. Bear in mind, however, that this was no pink Schwinn girls' bike. No...it was more like something straight out of the Wizard of Oz...like that old bike that mean old lady rode around. Still, it was transportation that enabled me off the property and into a play world of my own for an hour or two.

One event I clearly recall was the day Grandma took us over to meet a friend of hers who was 100 years old. Oh, Dear God! "Please, Grandma." I would beg. "Don't make me go into that house to see HER. She is old...and her house smells...and old people like that SCARE me!" Trust me, they truly did. Anyone that old from my 10-year-old perspective already had one foot in the grave and was just a whisper away from being a ghostly apparition. Little did I know that those visits would prepare me for a life with a Grandma who would live even BEYOND 100 years of age! While those in their "progressive" years like Grandma no longer frighten me, I am still reminded of the smell I sensed when I was young. My three young sons will tell me after they visit with "GiGi" that she smells, well, old. I don't say that to be offensive or mean. I just note that to put into perspective what a 10-year-old senses when put into a situation with someone 90 years older or more.

DON'T BE A QUITTER!

I was at an event one afternoon with several other parents and their kids. It was just an afternoon of fun in the sun and ice cream to celebrate the end of our boys' championship baseball season.

I tend to be one who sits quietly for a while, tuning in a "cocktail ear" to a neighboring conversation. Before you cry, "Eavesdropper," I prefer to think of it as the gathering of public information, and from there, I shall report on it. After all, if they did not want it to be heard, especially by those of us with incredible hearing, then they should not speak at all!

What I gathered from my "investigation," was that most of these ladies in their 30s and 40s arguably had some bodily complaint or another. I am sure most of it with good cause, but I still find it amusing. Call me lucky or call me the recipient of blessed genes, but I can scarcely recall a time when I had true physical complaints about my joints and all.

Evidently, the gals in question were discussing their recent workout routines, but the common thread was how "this leg hurt" or "this ankle is sore." Again, I am not mocking the reality of their situation. What I wish I could bestow upon them is some "grandmotherly advice." (Not from me....too young to go down that road yet, but from one of my best teachers ever: Grandma Kora.)

Grandma has been keen on physical activity for as long as I can remember. From swimming to cycling to leg lifts, exercise has been a mainstay in her life, and it continues to be! There was never an "I can't do that" or "That hurts too much to do that." She just simply did it! I am convinced that the discipline to do this daily kept the pain away!

In fact, when she was in her mid-60s, she attempted snow skiing for the first time. After she gracefully, and without incident, swooshed down the glistening slope, Grandma raised her poles triumphantly in the air to announce her "victory" to those of us watching her. That victory was soon to be dissolved, as within seconds, some guy without the obvious knowledge of understanding how to stop on skis, plowed into Grandma, sending her plunging to the ground, face in the snow. Long story short, she broke her leg.

Here is the interesting part. Grandma was rushed to the hospital and put through the usual requisite medical drills. By the next day, she was in a cast, but she was walking down the hallway in the hospital with crutches! Even in her mid-60s, this was no excuse to cry out in pain and give up. She simply resumed her activities, temporarily aided by crutches and a cast, but she never used it as an excuse to quit. She has never used anything as an excuse to quit. Heaven knows I have wanted to throw in the towel on occasion with certain things, but when I think about Grandma, and all of the times she might have had good cause to complain, she did not. How can I?

THE 70-MILE PUNISHMENT

When Grandma gives you a mandate, you listen! One particular story has been circling the family for years....decades....and it involves my Uncle Blaine, Grandma's youngest son, born in 1935. He vividly recalls being on the receiving end of her strict discipline back in the late 1940s. Bear in mind, this approach to a child not listening to a parent today would probably end up with Social Services knocking on the front door. But this particular era was different, and maybe, just maybe, sometimes we wish it could be the same today. Kids did not make the rules. They played by them, and if they didn't, then this particular scenario might have played out.

"We went to voice lessons every Saturday in Salina, a town less than an hour away from Russell," my uncle began. "One day, I was not where I was supposed to be when Mom was going to pick me up after my lesson. She didn't even give me one extra minute. I was not there on time, so she left without me. I had to hitch-hike 70 miles back home!"

As Uncle Blaine, then around 14 years old, began lumbering along Highway 40, heading west towards his home, no doubt wondering what additional punishment would greet him at the door once he arrived there. He did admit to feeling a bit nervous, but he knew this was the consequence of failing to report to Grandma on time.

"I not only walked down the main highway, but I also took some back roads to keep it interesting and to keep myself off the busy road. I would walk a bit, and then get picked up by some farmer who would drive me a few miles, and then I was back to walking again until I got another ride for a short distance," my uncle noted.

As for the cornucopia of emotions he was feeling that long afternoon, the dominant one was remorse over his own actions, not those of his mother.

"Sure, I was scared walking those 70 miles, but I was not upset at my mom. She expected me to be punctual, and I failed in that regard in this particular instance. It's a walk I will never forget."

Life lesson: When you are feeling emotionally wounded, be prepared to just walk it off! Some of us just have to walk more miles than others.

IT'S ALL IN THE CARDS!

Poker. Bridge. Kings on the Corner. If a deck of cards was involved, Grandma was all over it. In fact, Grandma even indulged her interest in this passion on my wedding day in 1993. In the hour before I said "I do," Grandma caught a few of the groomsmen huddled over a deck of cards in one of the pews towards the rear of the church. First interested in what all the fuss was about, Grandma approached them. Maybe she'd hone in on some incredible secret, or, at the very least, hear a dirty joke worthy of repeating.

When she stood over this group of four young men, she discovered they were playing cards, presumably poker or black jack. Due to the nature of the circumstances....it was my wedding day, after all....and they were in God's house, Grandma advised them (interpret the word "advised" as you will!) to put the cards away, but as the story later goes, evidently Grandma told them she'd hook up with them at the reception to carry on in the game.

According to numerous sources who have known Grandma over the years, she loved to play cards...still does. Her specialties have always been bridge and poker, and her gang of card playing buddies always played for pennies, sometimes dollars. High rollers, they were!

One resident of her home town recalls his parents playing weekly with Grandma and her gang.

"One particular time, I came along with my parents and sat in on the game," the fellow noted. "Boy! Is she ever competitive! I saw her thrust her elbow into my dad's rib cage during the game. The stakes were high, too. You put in one dollar. She hosted that weekly poker club for years. The men eventually died off, leaving just the women to gather and play. A couple of the guys held on for a bit, but I think they grew rather weary of Kora's fierce competitiveness. If you did not know the game and if you did not play well, she didn't want you there."

According to this gentleman, Grandma was always determined, always on a mission.

He laughed and noted, "My mom used to always warn me about Kora, especially when Kora was driving through town. One particular day, as I was riding in the car with my mom, I suddenly heard my mom scream, 'Look out! Here comes Kora! She is going to pull right into the post office parking lot.' Sure enough, she did, taking the first available spot, hopping out of the car, and heading right into the post office, never missing a beat. People just sort of learned to stay out of her way."

That same intense focus is to what I give credit for my flat chest today! Seriously! When I was a kid, shoulder seat belts did not exist; only lap ones did, and they were not often used. I would frequently sit shot gun next to Grandma as she drove, the pedal fiercely to the metal, and whenever she came to an abrupt stop, her right arm would instinctively shoot straight out perpendicular to her body and across my chest to keep me from bowing into the dash board. After several formative years of riding with her and experiencing the first-ever "Grandma's arm seat belt," I am convinced she somewhat deprived me of an hour-glass figure in my northern hemisphere region.

NOT EVEN HARD-EARNED CELEBRITY STATUS COULD KEEP YOU FROM RESPECTING – AND SOMETIMES FEARING! – GRANDMA KORA!

Among the prominent and successful individuals who had his roots in Russell was Wendall Anschutz, a well-known, talented, and highly-respected news anchor for over a quarter of a century in the Kansas City market, working for KCTV 5 news. Sadly, he passed away in 2010 from cancer. He is greatly missed and will always be remembered as a significant part of Kansas City's history, and one who never forgot his small-town beginnings.

A few years ago, I connected with Wendall and we enjoyed a few lunches together as we reminisced about Grandma and her ways. In his 70s at the time of our meetings, Wendall still carried with him strong impressions of my grandmother.

"She was my cub scout leader back in the 1940s," he noted. "She was really into it, too. She'd come to the meetings all decked out in her uniform and all. Everything she did, no matter how small or how big, she took seriously."

He continued to tell me things I already suspected, but it was entertaining to hear them from a different voice other than that in my own head, fully created by my own impressions – and theories – about Grandma.

"Everyone in this town of about 7,000 people knew Kora. It was almost impossible not to know who she was," he emphasized. "Lloyd (my grandfather) was the quieter one of the two. I suspect he just never had the opportunity to ever get a word in. He just kind of sat back and let Kora do her thing. He figured he did not have much say in it anyway. He did sit on the city council with my dad, though. Perhaps he found through that an outlet to finally have his voice heard!"

Wendall recalled his mom coming home once from a bridge party that Grandma had attended, and it was pretty evident that Grandma let her voice be heard at that event, too.

"My mom bolted through the front door in tears when she got home because Kora had gotten after her for not playing the game well that day. When it came to Kora and bridge, you had to play the game well and play it by the rules. There was no room for messing up."

There was no messing up, either, when it came to hanging out with your friends and staying out of trouble.

"Back in the 1940s, there were several street gangs in Russell," said Wendall. "There was the second street gang, the third street gang, and the fourth street gang."

Now I hardly suspect that these "street gangs' carried with them shot guns and knives. If anything, they probably had sling shots and BB guns. Evidently, my dad was on the second street gang and was the ring leader in more than one small-town, backyard, boys-on-the-prowl incident. According to Wendall, one afternoon my dad snuck into my grandpa's pharmacy to get some sulfur that would later be used to make stink bombs, which they threw over fences at other gangs.

In one particular incident, Wendall witnessed my dad and his gang, all around age 12 or 13 at the time, grab a boy from another gang and bring him into my grandparents' detached garage that was out back behind the house. They had no intentions of actually hanging the kid. They just wanted to playfully scare him. As they wrestled together, three or four of them, they finally managed to hang the boy up on some hook by his shirt collar, along with some rope.

"That boy soon turned blue in the face, and as the other boys hurriedly tried to get the boys down, Kora just so happened to walk by and immediately cut that rope and got the boy down," Wendall recalled.

I am certain that after that particular incident, my dad, usually the better-behaved of Grandma's boys, had to endure some sort of unpleasant discipline rendered by Grandma. I am also certain that was the last of his street gang days.

THE SECRET TO RAISING SUCCESSFUL CHILDREN

During one of my radio interviews with Grandma, I inquired of her as to what her secret was to raising such successful kids. After all, both of her boys excelled not only academically and athletically, but also in matters of professional endeavors.

I have read countless books on the matter, pored over numerous articles that speak to the subject, in hopes of finding "the answer" to an age-old question.

I could have saved myself a lot of time, money, and energy, if I had only consulted the original source in the first place.

Me: What is your secret to raising such successful boys?

Grandma: (Without skipping a beat) That's easy. They had a successful mother!

Enough said!

WHEN GOD CALLS YOU HOME, THAT'S ALL PART OF THE PLAN. ACCEPT IT!

September 27, 1990

Too bad about Justine being so bad off, but Susan should just understand that this is life and we all have to go sometime, and it isn't any easier if it would be now or ten years from now, and also that her kids will probably have to be doing the same thing. That just is life, and we have to understand it and cope with it.

That was an excerpt of a letter Grandma wrote to me when I was living in Dallas. At the time, my maternal grandmother, Justine, was very ill and subsequently died four months later. My mom had been struggling with that particular passage of life, and Grandma was very aware of it. However, Grandma just had a way of dealing with life as it should naturally flow.

She once told me, "Sure, when someone you love dies, you miss them. Why wouldn't you? But you have to go on. They would want you to go on. In fact, when I die, if I find out you cried, I'll be angry. I want you to have a big celebration. A party. Eat all day long. Celebrate! I had a great life! Don't cry because I'm gone. If you do cry, cry because you're still here and I'm in Heaven. Don't shed a dang tear for me, or I'll come back to haunt you. I mean it. Ya hear me?"

YOU HAVE TO LOOK OUT FOR YOURSELF, TOO

May 27, 1991:

Dear Ann:

I hear you told your folks that they had turned off the lights for Joe, as he hadn't paid his bills and maybe he hadn't paid his rent, either. Well, now quit worrying about him. He wants it that way. He prefers his drugs to light, rent, and you. So forget him! I hope you don't ever leave him in the house, or give him a chance to push himself in, because when people want money for drugs, they will do anything for it, even kill for $10.00. I hope you know that. They get crazed and don't know what they are doing. So please be careful.

Even now if Joe would change and get off drugs, it is too late. You could never feel secure, thinking constantly that he might revert back to it. You'd better get that divorce before he is ever put in prison or else you'd always have to say your husband was in prison. If you do it before, you will never have to say that. Think that over. Get on with your life and start living. Some of your troubles at work could be from all of this stress you are under, too, did you ever think of that? Some of it might be your fault. Stress is hard on anyone.

So, think it over. I just want the best for you. I love you. Take heart. Write me.

Grdma H

P.S. – Get your name back when you get divorced – Hollinger!

When I was living in Dallas in the early 1990s, I was going to school and working at a law firm as a paralegal. My husband at that time, whom I divorced six months after this letter was written, had become addicted to drugs and in the process became quite abusive, uncontrollable, and highly unpredictable. It was a horrible situation for me. I struggled with the thought of divorce initially. As a strong Christian, I did not feel it was the right thing to do. I took those words, "til death do us part" quite seriously.

Fortunately, between heavy internal contemplation, as well as taking the advisement of several friends and family members into consideration, I severed my ties with the man. And, yes, I did have my maiden name restored, in a highly interesting fashion.

My maternal grandpa, Washington "Wash" Brown, was an attorney. He was more than willing to handle my divorce proceedings, as he never really cared much for my soon-to-be ex in the first place. He was a legal hound who had just been thrown a biscuit, and it was chow time!

After deciding to leave my husband, I called my dad and asked if he would come get me, packed up all of my belongings, and as soon as my dad made the long drive from Kansas City to Dallas in the station wagon, we loaded up my car and his car and headed north towards home.

I had barely returned home when my grandpa, 85 years old at the time, initiated the divorce action. Within 24 hours, he had my case on the docket and called me to say, "Get to the courthouse immediately."

When I arrived in the courtroom and my case number was called, I walked up to the bench and sat in the stand to the left of the judge. Was I nervous? Not really. I was just eager to get this over with and move on with my life. I'd never been in this position before, and I sincerely hoped I never would again.

Grandpa soon approached the bench and paced slowly back and forth as he interrogated me. Although I had always known him to dress well, complete with bow tie and hat, his outer appearance that day was somewhat intimidating to me. I presume he merely wanted to add some theatrics to this occasion to have his literal day in court. After all, his granddaughter was severing all ties with a man whom he despised.

As he pontificated and presented a host of mundane questions relevant to the case, one of his final questions took me off-guard.

"Did you or did you not marry the Respondent without the approval of your grandfather?" he inquired of me, rather officially, I might add, his courtroom eyes barreling into mine.

I mumbled a bit, uncertain as to how I should answer that question, and wondering if my response would in one way or another determine the outcome of my case. I had seen too many legal shows on TV and was beginning to sweat. I shot a quick glance at the court reporter who suddenly gained interest in her job. This was turning into a soap opera before my very eyes. A hush blanketed the courtroom, all eyes upon me, wondering just how I would answer such an unexpected inquiry.

Not receiving an answer from me, he repeated the question: "Did you or did you not marry the Respondent without the approval of your grandfather?"

The jokester in me wanted to ask, "Of which grandfather are you speaking?" After all, I did have two of them. Yes...one had died years earlier, but it was a legitimate query in my opinion.

As Grandpa came in closer to hear my response, I lowered my head in shame and said, "Yes. Yes I suppose I did."

I never saw such a grin of affirmation in my life as the one that decorated his face in that moment.

After a few more routine questions, Grandpa approached the judge and cited, "Your honor. I respectfully approach the bench and ask that my granddaughter's maiden name be restored...effective immediately."

The judge's gavel hit his desk. Case closed. Grandpa was happy. Grandma got her wish, as well. I was back to being a Hollinger.

Interestingly enough, the fun did not stop there for Grandpa. When he returned home later that evening, he took my wedding photo off his living room wall, removed the nearly two-year-old picture from the frame, and ever-so-carefully cut my ex-husband's presence out of the photo. He then replaced the photo back in the frame, carefully putting it back on the wall where it originally hung. After all, he mused, it was still a good photo. It was even better now. It remained there til the day he died.

AND THE WEATHER FORECAST CALLS FOR PARTLY SUNNY SKIES WITH AN OCCASIONAL MICROBURST!

Grandma has always rolled with the punches. She never let much ruffle her feathers. Well, I take that back. She does let things bother her, but her secret to dealing with stress is to not continually dwell upon things. She has her say in something, shows appropriate emotion over it, and then moves on. She's always been this way, and it is to this that I attribute her longevity and good health. She does not internalize her stress. She blows it away. She bursts its' bubble.

One spring day in 2010, my husband and I made the four hour drive from Kansas City to Russell to visit grandma for the weekend. We advised the woman who at the time looked in on Grandma throughout the day that we would arrive at Grandma's house around five in the evening, give or take. Grandma, however, likes punctuality and precise times. There's no give or take. If you say you are going to be somewhere at five, then you are there precisely at five. That's simply being true to your word. Grandma does not like to waste time, either.

In this particular instance, however, my husband and I inadvertently arrived about 30 minutes late. When we walked into Grandma's house, we found her sitting on the divan in her front room, obviously emotionally exhausted, and the first words out of her mouth, as she cried and visibly shook, were, "Oh, my god! There you are. I have been worried sick about you. I pictured you two dead on the highway with your suitcases all over the road. I thought your car had crashed. I then imagined how many calls I would have to make to friends and family telling them about the funerals and everything. Just imagine how many people's schedules that would affect."

My husband and I just stood there and listened to her rampage. In less than five minutes, it was over, nearly forgotten, and replaced with an enthusiastic, "Now, let's go to dinner. I'm hungry."

It was at that time that my husband coined a new word for those brief emotional outbursts of Grandma's: microbursts. Just as quickly and emphatically as they come, they are gone! They elicit a brief emotional disturbance, and then quickly fade.

Microbursts. Those sure do sound far more appealing than dwelling on something for days, weeks, months, or even years. Let it all out in an instant, and then be done with it! Your body cannot hang on to the negativity during a microburst. It reacts and then blows it away with a proactive frame of mind. After her microbursts, Grandma just gets on with living. After all, on this particular evening, a hot meal awaited her! What could be better than that?

MY DEAREST LLOYD

LLOYD L. HOLLINGER, AGE 26 (1927)

Russell, Kansas

July 25, 1927

My dearest Lloyd:

Guess I better hurry and write this letter and take it down and mail it so you won't miss out a day. I fared pretty well today. Got your special delivery at 7 bells this morning. Too bad I didn't get it yesterday. Then, I got your other letter after arriving home this evening - was about 6:45, and well I needed one. I was that blue.

Changed my first tire today and that was coming home out here to London's. Sure had a time, too. I sure thought about you then – so see how much I need you and depend on you? Gosh, I'll be glad when I get back "home" to you. Carrie will be back Wednesday, she says. Peanuts and Grace say they are going back with me and Peanuts can't be gone Saturday and I asked her this even if she would want to leave Saturday after she got off work, or we could leave early Sunday morn. Let me know which. Should we go by nite? Or leave early in the morn? Write me honey!

I wrote a check today for $5.00, which leaves

a balance of $248.67. Just now I looked in my purse. I didn't have much money when I arrived in Great Bend. Bought some stuff which amounted to $0.44 and wrote a check for $5.00, so now I have $6.00. The lady that changed my money must have short-changed herself. That's pretty good.

I'm sure a sick kid. Got one heck of a cold. Everyone says it's hay fever. All I do is blow my nose and sneeze. My nose is so sore and my head feels so stuffy. Kids want to go swimming tonight. I don't know if I will. Might go along, though. Peanuts is having club tomorrow nite. Having us kids to the Hotel Russell to dinner in the eve. Don't know what we'll do afterwards. Oh, lord, I'm so lonesome for you!!

Guess your folks are moving today. Will go out before I leave. Seems like I've been home for weeks.

Well, sweetheart, will close. Love me lots as I love you. Hope to see you soon, honey.

Yours!

Kora

Shortly after Grandma and Grandpa were married in early 1927, Grandpa took an internship of sorts in Oklahoma to hone his skills as a pharmacist before coming back to Russell to open his own drug store. During this time, they were routinely separated, as Grandma frequently returned to Russell to prepare things for their new life back in their home town of Russell.

As one who was fond of writing letters and who used them as her primary form of communication, Grandma resorted to writing to her "Lloydie" nearly every day during this particular time of their life together. She loved that man so much. She was all of 22 years old. He would be 26 that year. I've only known my grandma as "Grandma," so reading the box of letters I found that she had lovingly penned to my grandfather was very special. She, too, was young once, and something so many of us forget when we interact with the elderly. They all have stories. They all have a vibrant youth to relive in their minds. One day, it will be us who will move into the dusk of our lives and wonder where those years went. Will people remember our stories? Will they want to learn from our experiences? Will our presence have made a difference?

Now, more than ever, it is important to reach out to those generations of brave individuals who have blazed the trail before you. From wagon wheels to hybrid cars, the path has never been easy, but the journey for everyone should be worth noting. As Grandma has always told me, "Everything happens for a reason. You may not know now. You may not know next week. You may not even know until you're old. Doesn't matter. Everything has a purpose and reason. Just appreciate the magic in that."

As you follow your own path in life, be sure to make tracks in the road. It lets people know you were there. When you do, the tracks you leave behind will remain in the hearts and minds of others for years to come.

COUNTING SHEEP IS FOR SISSIES! DO THE MATH INSTEAD!

When my dad and his brother were of school age, Grandma used to quiz them every night before they fell asleep. She would sit on the edge of their beds and begin a little chant such as the following:

"What is 2 x 2 + 6 + 4 -3 + 8 x 5...." You get the picture. She would do this until one of the boys got it right, although my uncle swears that at times, Grandma just made up an answer so the boys would settle down and fall asleep quickly!

A DOG THAT PRAYED

Grandma and Grandpa had an amazing dog named Snoopy. Snoopy, basically a mutt, owned the town. He knew his place in life and was not about to let anyone mess with that. This dog would hang out on the front porch of Grandma's house or outside the pharmacy they owned. I suppose they should have called their pharmacy "Hollinger and Snoopy Drug."

Snoopy even had a spiritual essence about him. He actually attended church every Sunday, without fail. Even when my grandparents, dad, and uncle were out of town, Snoopy would hear those church bells ring on Sunday morning, alerting him that it was time to worship. As the first bell tolled, he would dash the few blocks from home to sit just outside the church door to spend time in worship with the other parishioners. He obviously had his priorities in life.

His denomination of choice: The Methodist Church, of course!

In the name of the Father, the Son, and the Holy Dog!

WISE WORDS FROM A PROUD FATHER (ALWAYS GO FOR THE GOLD IN LIFE....IT STARTS WITH BEING A WINNER IN YOUR HEART!)

I once asked Grandma why she has always been so confident in life and so seemingly self-assured. Her answer to that inquiry both shocked and amazed me. Back in 1910, when Grandma was just five years old, she recalls her dad sitting down with her one particular evening and telling her as he intently focused his gaze into her eyes, "Kora," he began. "I want you to know that there is nothing in life you cannot accomplish if you have the genuine desire to do so. Desire and determination, coupled with the willingness to do the work to reach your goals, trump everything else. If you want to do something and know you can do it, then get out there and do it. Remember that, and you will go far."

For the record, Grandma has never once doubted herself or her abilities, and she would be the first to remind me if I ever mentally got off track.

Her dedication to this train of belief was still fully evident as I posed a question to her during one of my talk radio shows a few years ago. At the time, the summer Olympics were in full swing. Grandma, then age 103, began to reminisce about her sporting days when she was younger, commenting on how well she performed in various track and field events and in basketball games.

Always confident in herself and filled with purpose, Grandma contemplated on what could have been her athletic glory days, "You know; I wish I would have entered into the Olympic games back in the day. I wish I could do it now. I know for sure that I could perform just as well as, if not better than, those athletes of today. You're darn right I could."

Confidence. If it works for Grandma, it can work for you, too. Believe in yourself, and you can always take home the gold! Just remember to keep it in your heart forever!

"AIN'T LOVE GRAND?"

Grandma loved it whenever one of her grandkids moved to another city, as this gave her a perfect excuse to pack her bags and get away for a while. She loved visiting all of us grandkids, no matter where we lived as we pursued our adult lives.

In 1987, I decided to take a leap of faith and head out to southern California to pursue a career in the film industry. When Grandma got wind of this relocation endeavor, she immediately made plans to come out and stay with me for a week. On the day she arrived, I met her at Los Angeles International Airport, excited about the next seven days ahead, as when Grandma puts her mind to it, a vacation is a whirlwind of constant activity and excitement. Definitely not for relaxing.

I enthusiastically greeted her as she disembarked from the plane and into the terminal. I had barely given her a hug when her eyes caught something that intrigued her. Barely 100 yards away from us was a young couple, probably about my age, maybe a bit younger. They were dressed in punk rock clothing, as was popular at the time. The boy had spiked, black hair, chains on his tight-fitting black jeans, with a black and white striped shirt. The young girl had a punk hairstyle with the colors of the rainbow in it, and you could hang more ornaments from her ears than you could from a Christmas tree. As many body piercings as she had, I imagined that if she drank a bottle of water, she'd take on the presence of a sprinkler.

After my brief hug with Grandma, she marched right over to this young couple.

"Oh, no!" I worried. "Is she going to embarrass me? Is she going to utter some comment that will make them turn on us, and then out of nowhere comes their entire gang?"

I watched her dutifully walk the 100 yards or so to the young couple, now embraced in a steady lip lock.

"Not good timing, Grandma. Definitely not good timing," I muttered, as I followed close behind her, grabbing her carry-on bag on the way.

By the time I reached Grandma, she was tapping the young man on the shoulder from behind. I think she had to tap more than once, as the boy obviously had other things on his mind at the time and appeared oblivious to the old lady standing right behind him. Grandma once again tapped the boy on the shoulder. He then released his hold from the girl, turned his head to the side and then down towards Grandma, and all she had to say in the face of his dumbfounded look was, "Ain't love grand?"

That was it! She then walked away! She had no intention of saying anything other than, "Ain't love grand?" Punk hair, tight clothes, body piercings...none of that fazed her. She just wanted to remind this couple probably 60 years her junior that love is special.

As we walked away, I glanced back over my shoulder and saw those two kids just look at us, saying nothing. I would like to believe that to this day, whether that couple is still in contact or not, that they recall the day when a blue-haired granny approached them in the airport and reminded them of the beauty of love.

WHO SAYS YOU HAVE TO GROW OLD?

The world is full of anti-aging products, secrets, tips, and illusions, but if you truly want to feel remarkably years younger in an instant, then stand next to a gal well into her 100s and see how you feel! The simple fact that she is of such a mature age does not make you feel younger in and of itself. The fact that she is still full of life makes you feel younger, almost as if you have years ahead of you, no matter what your age.

I had to remind myself of this fact while at a meeting one morning a couple of years ago. A younger man in the group, around age 27, pointed out that I was, well, older than he is. Yes, at 45, I was older, but that does not make me OLD. He was implying that I would probably be retiring within a few years. What???? I don't know what his generation is thinking, but in my world, we never retire. People in my family are still employed at the time of their demise. My grandfather was into his nineties when he passed away, yet he was, up until a few months prior to his death, heading out to the office every day, just as he had done for nearly 70 years. My uncle, age 76, works full-time as a medical doctor. I truly believe that his energy and work ethic have kept him young. You would never be able to tell at first glance that he is approaching 80. I guarantee you that the young man who noted I would probably be retiring in a few years will be retired well before I will even think about it!

So, let's get back to standing next to an elderly lady. (No, you are not standing next to me. Picture my granny here. Focus!) One hot summer day in July 2009, I had the honor of meeting her at the airport on her return trip from the east coast. She had a three-hour layover before her "puddle jumper" plane escorted her back to her small town in the Midwest. This gave Grandma and my husband and I the opportunity to spend some quality time with each other. All I can say is that Grandma surely can make all of us look bad when it comes to living life to the fullest!

For most senior citizens, the term "aging well" includes having a healthy body, an active mind, a healthy lifestyle, and a positive attitude. For Grandma, that means check, check, check, and double-check! She fits all of those criteria, and more! In 2004, a team of researchers from the University of Texas conducted a study that revealed, unsurprisingly, that "people with an upbeat view of life were less likely than pessimists to show signs of frailty." Their findings suggested that people who held fast to a positive outlook on life were much less likely to become frail. Grandma has that one nailed down.

After we picked her up at the airport and retrieved her belongings from the baggage claim, we headed over to the adjacent terminal to find a place to grab a bite to eat and just chat before her connecting flight departed. The airport gave Grandma the use of a wheelchair as a courtesy. (I am wondering if for legal reasons, they give these to anyone who looks over 50!) Grandma could have walked on her own, but I think she enjoyed putting me to work, telling me to pull over at the nearest eating establishment! At the rate she was requiring me to hustle, I was afraid I might get pulled over for speeding!

We found a place to grab a bite to eat. During our lunch, Grandma began to pontificate about life.

"You know," she began. "I keep thinking about Heaven. I mean, how do they possibly have room for all of those people up there?"

I never thought about it that way and asked her, "What do you mean? There is plenty of room. I am sure of that."

"No," she continued. "I just don't see how there could be much more room up there now. I suppose I have to wait around to die until they kick a few out."

She took a slurp of her soup and then said, "And I certainly do not intend to head in the opposite direction when I die!" Leave it to Grandma to have such a delicate reference to Hell.

Since we were on the topic, I asked her who she would probably see first in Heaven, provided they cleared out the clutter first.

"Oh, I suppose I would see Lloyd and L.A.," she expressed, in reference to her late husband who passed away 30 years ago and to my late father, her oldest son, who died in 1993 just a few weeks shy of his 60th birthday.

"Do you think they will let Uncle Blaine up there when he dies?" I joked.

Not missing a beat and recognizing the orneriness of her then 74-year-old, very energetic son, Grandma replied, "They may not want him!" Then she laughed that all-out guffaw for which she is known by family and friends. If you are sitting or standing near her when she laughs, you could get sprayed! Bring some wipes.

After lunch, her sweet tooth kicked in. She was on the prowl for some chocolate or a big cinnamon roll with all of the calories smeared over it. At her age, calories are the least of her worries! (Wouldn't that be great?) She is not large; yet eating is her favorite sport. "If I can't eat it, I don't want it," she will respond when asked what she wants for her birthday. "I'll eat anything."

I have heard that a sense of humor keeps the years off of a person, too. No wonder Grandma is still rocking it! At one point during our airport stay, we got a bit bored. I had an idea and asked Grandma if she would be willing to participate. I did not have to ask her twice.

We decided that I would sit in the wheelchair and she would push ME! She got up out of the chair and I plopped my hindquarters in it. She stood behind it and

began pushing me down the terminal. Between fits of laughter, I had to yell, "Grandma! Slow down! You're scaring me!" My husband had the foresight to break out the camera at this point. Since I was thus caught on film "abusing" a geriatric, I then made my husband get in the chair, and, yes, Grandma pushed HIM! The looks we got from people ran from general intrigue to "what's the number for the geriatric abuse hotline?" It was, in true fashion, a Borat-like moment! And Grandma loved it! She was smiling the whole time because she knows that she is named in MY will and that, with her active and upbeat lifestyle, she quite possibly could outlive me.

Once we put the wheelchair aside, she asked me, "So, how about a cruise next summer?"

That is yet another way to avert the aging process. Make plans to live for...and live a life that others would die for! Just make sure you keep a comfortable place up in Heaven for Grandma one of these years!

DON'T SLOW DOWN...THAT WILL JUST AGE YOU!

Grandma has always enjoyed writing letters to family members over the years, usually rambling on and on about her busy agenda. It has been through that active social climate that her energy and resolve to keep on living have been continually fueled. Check out this little note mailed to her grandson in 2003, when she was just a young thing of 98 years old:

Busy week. Tonight I have bridge club; tomorrow night is a church meeting. Wednesday night I plan to take my neighbors to the north of me to McDonald's for pancakes. Been wanting to do this for two years, so hope I can, too. Will have to give up my usual gang that day. Thursday night is Poker Club. Friday night is a party and Saturday is the KU game. Is that enough? Well, take care. Hope we can beat Missouri on Saturday, but I have my doubts!

Love,

Grdma H

Grandma resists the "idle" life so she can enjoy an "ideal" life! Try it! You may have years of enjoyment ahead of you!

REALIZE THE ONE SIMPLE TECHNIQUE THAT MAKES YOU GLOW.

It is never too late to understand that the one beauty secret is literally right under your nose. According to Grandma, you should never leave the house without the greatest of accessories: your smile....and make it genuine! (Be sure the lipstick stains are off of your teeth, too! Major fashion blunder!)

FIND THE JOY IN THE ART OF CONVERSATION WITH ANOTHER FRIENDLY SOUL...EVEN IF HE CANNOT UNDERSTAND A DANG WORD YOU ARE SAYING. AT LEAST YOU'VE SPOKEN!

While vacationing in Germany in the 1980s to visit her grandson who was temporarily residing there, Grandma managed to strike up a conversation with an elderly German man for whom English was not even an option at that time in his life. Seemingly unaware that her companion in conversation knew not a word of English, Grandma still chatted with him for about an hour as if he was an old friend with whom she needed to catch up. For Grandma, it was one of the best dialogues she had ever enjoyed...or perhaps I should say "monologue."

DON'T LET THE BUFFET SNEEZE GUARDS REMAIN A DETERRENT!

Buffets and Grandma. They go together like salt and pepper, like Christmas and Santa. Grandma loves a good buffet, which is one reason she loves cruises. "Midnight buffet or early morning breakfast? Which way do I turn?" she mused on one particular Caribbean cruise. (She did both! You only live once!)

Now, if you are like most people, when you go through a buffet line, you respect the sneeze guard. It's there for a reason. For Grandma, however, it simply gets in the way. She has no problem with putting her head down under that guard and checking out the goods. "That's better," she'll note. "I can see what's under here now." She will then proceed to pick at a few things to see if she might want to load those up on her plate. For germ freaks out there, this is when you learn that doing the buffet thing with Grandma requires you go *in front* of her and make sure the "all you can eat" invitation means that you better grab all you can eat in one trip through the buffet. I suggest you just let her follow along behind you. By the time she gets to the end of the buffet line, she has practically had a full meal, what with all of the sampling and all.

However, despite what some folks might view as just plain rude and definitely not hygienic, Grandma does illustrate a point in her actions. When you want something in life, go for it! No matter how small or big the desire. Even when dining at the local buffet, if you are not sure you want something, dip your head under the sneeze guard, grab a piece of food between your thumb and forefinger, place it in your mouth, and then decide if it is worth pursuing. Even in life, grab a little taste of it to see if you want to take part in that endeavor. Always pursue your life's desires, even if you have to sample them first. How are you ever going to know if you like it or not?

Grandma always, always told us to try everything at least once...food, an experience, you name it. Then, make a decision as to whether or not you like it. Sometimes, you realize you are right – you didn't like it. Other times, you just may surprise yourself and find something you never even knew you had a taste for.

ALWAYS KNOW HOW TO DRESS YOURSELF!

Even at her age, Grandma knows when to kick in the party attitude. While vacationing with the rest of her family at a luxury cabin in Colorado a couple summers ago, she decided it was time for a hot tub party. While the others were doing their own thing in the living room, Grandma snuck off and put on her bathing suit, then came back and made a grand

entrance back into the main area, proudly announcing, "I'm ready for some fun! Who's going to join me?" After someone handed her a margarita, Grandma headed off to the spa and had the time of her life. The extra salt on the rim of the glass was an added treat. (Now if only the hot tub had been filled with salt water!)

BRAG ABOUT THE KIDS OR GRANDKIDS....AS INSIGHTFULLY AS POSSIBLE!

"That Ann," Grandma told a friend recently. "She is a great gal, but she can't cook worth a lick. Just ask her skinny husband over there."

TAKE THE STAIRS EVERY CHANCE YOU GET. DON'T TAKE THE ELEVATOR!

At a friend's funeral back in 2007 ("You go to a lot of funerals when you are my age," quipped Grandma) when she was just a young thing of 102, Grandma entered the funeral home and the director escorted her to the elevator. Somewhat insulted, she promptly told him, "I don't need to take the elevator. Those are for old folks! I'll take the stairs, thank you!"

KEEP ON GRINNING!

Be sure to flash those pearly whites no matter where you go....just be sure to brush and floss first. However, if you have crossed the threshold of 100 years, we may politely overlook that neglected habit. (Hey! At 106 years old, she still has her own teeth! No fake ones here!)

GRANDMA KORA, ENJOYING HER 29TH CARIBBEAN CRUISE, JULY 2010.

TRAVEL LIGHTLY? DEPENDS ON THE JOURNEY, BUT BE ORGANIZED ABOUT IT!

Even at age 102, Grandma still did things her way. When a friend was lending a helping hand as Grandma packed her suitcases for yet another fun adventure, Grandma grew increasingly impatient and frustrated with how her friend was packing her bags. So, she quickly took matters into her own hands....or, knees, if you will, and got down on the floor and spent the next 15 minutes on her knees organizing her three bags. One for the visit to Susan's house. One for the visit to Blaine's house. One for the trip to the mountains. Each bag had its purpose. Heaven forbid the underwear meant to be worn at Susan's house ended up in the bag deemed for the mountain vacation.

Here is another letter written by Grandma to friends and family as she hopped the Atlantic to explore parts of Europe. She's never at a loss for being very descriptive about her travels, is she? Please...read on!

September 1977   5 p.m. New York

Dear One and All:

Will start a letter now. Arrive here about 4:30 p.m......have gotten our seats, called Sadie and Bill and now waiting 'til our plane leaves at 6:50, and I don't think we will be very happy with it. Hear it's loaded and seats 3-3, so tight squeeze! That 1011 is great....2-4-2 seats and very roomy. Had snack between KC and Chicago....there one hour so

we got off and called Aunt Joe. We had a snack —
two sandwiches and coffee. Then between Chicago
and New York, another snack in a cute German
box....2 sandwiches and small package of candy,
some crackers and some cheese and a pretzel and
any drinks. Plane holds 263. Better than a 747.
Lloyd is strolling now and later I'll stroll. Will
write later.

8:30 p.m. — Still on the ground — planes can't
land in London — too much air traffic — have a
nice young girl seated with us. Menu has been
passed out but no food yet! I'm having barbeque
ribs and Lloyd is having breast of chicken — 3
choices — combination salad, coconut-raspberry
cake, peas, etc. — Hope we get going soon. More
later...

Well, we arrived in London at 8:30 London
time. 6 hrs. difference. Not much sleep. Met at
airport and no customs going through bags. Have
a lovely room — TV, radio, and all lights, etc.,
turn on from our twin beds. Big room and
bathroom, plenty of towels, soap — hope all our
motels are this nice....carpeted, AC, tub, shower.
Our towels are even heated! Plenty of hot water,

too. We have breakfast served in our room.

Sunday AM, 4:45 – Had to be up by 4:30 – this time only to catch plane to Amsterdam, Holland. Will have breakfast shortly. Had to have our bags out at 4:45. Took tour yesterday AM. In PM went to Harrods. Do you remember that, LA? Boy is that place huge and expensive! Had lunch there. Then last night went to a fancy place for dinner – pricewise- and good and then to Globe Theatre for "Donkeys' Years." Said been running here for two years. Wasn't too crazy about it. Called and talked to Frank's dad. Seemed very interesting over the phone. Will definitely mail this today so don't know when I'll write again. Just not time – have so many to send cards to, as well. So, Love, Mother. Have a nice group – 12 from Pueblo, two from St. Louis and two from Arkansas, Ohio, Indiana, Florida, Mass., Dallas.

Sun., 6:30 PM Just arrived in Brussels – a gorgeous drive, lovely roads – a great bus – seats across aisle staggered and what a hotel here in Brussels! Huge! Better than any we've stayed in over in the states. We have TWO stools in the bathroom! And L.A., we've also had 110 V for razor.

Please let Wash and Justine read this — no time for writing — and then could you mail it to Sarah...and then Sarah, would you then mail it on to Pearl and Pearl can you let Kathryn, Leona, and Opal read it, too? I'll really appreciate this.

Getting to eat dinner tonight in "Beefeater" room. Lloyd is doing real well, too.....our canal ride in Amsterdam was lovely and saw Ann Frank's home and church.

Love, Mother

APPRECIATE YOUR LIFE, BUT NEVER FEAR THE FINAL CHAPTER!

When Kora was 103, she dutifully attended a friend's funeral. As she made her way up to view the casket and looked down at the peaceful body that lay within, she told her dearly departed friend, "You're the lucky one now."

WASTE NOT, WANT NOT!

Not one to let the hallmarks of life, such as the death of a dear friend, slow her down, Grandma always appreciates opportunities to save a buck or two. After another friend's funeral (again, you have to understand, once you eclipse 100 years of age, funerals are just as regular events as trips to the bathroom!), Grandma inquired of the surviving relatives, who were going to donate the deceased's clothing to charity, if she could just have all of those clothes. "She's not gonna need them where she's going, and besides, she was the same size as me." That was over 20 years ago. Grandma still wears some of those outfits.

DON'T SWEAT THE HOT FLASHES!

Although menopause was decades ago, Grandma claims she never had one physical set back during those days. "Hot flash?" she hollered. "What's a hot flash? Never heard of 'em." The only time I have ever seen her sweat was when we spent some time in Houston one year. All she could say amidst the constant humidity was "I'm just wringing wet!" She was so worried about the lasting effects it would have on her hair.

FOLLOW THE RULES, BUT LIVE AS IF THEY WERE NOT DESIGNED FOR YOU!

When she was 100 years of age, Grandma was preparing to fly from Kansas City to Houston to visit her son. When she proceeded towards the terminal, she realized she had forgotten her photo ID. She was convinced, however, that since she was 100 years of age, airport personnel would just let it slide. In a post 9-11 world, no such chance. You just never know what an old bag might have in her old bag. Thank goodness she gave herself plenty of time to get to the airport before her flight departed, as someone had to drive from her small town over four hours away to meet Grandma's neighbor, who originally drove her to the airport that day, half-way to get the ID. Grandma was still growling as she boarded the plane, "Why do I need an ID? At 100 years of age, I don't have to prove to anyone who I am! I've been here long enough. They should know by now who I am!"

PLAN YOUR FUNERAL IN ADVANCE...YOU JUST NEVER KNOW WHEN YOU MIGHT NEED IT!

When she was in her 70s, Grandma began making arrangements for her what would one day be her funeral service. In typical Kora Hollinger fashion, she left nothing to chance. She picked out an outfit for each season so she would be properly dressed in the after-life. She interviewed potential pall bearers and even had the organists audition for her. What she learned over the next three decades is that as those players died off, she had to continually find replacements! It can be a killer planning your own funeral over a span of three, going on four, decades! "When your friends die and then THEIR kids begin to die off, you know you have been around a long, long time," says Grandma. Auditions are still being held. Apply within. One of Grandma's key questions will be, "So...how's your health?" She wants to make sure you will be at the ready when she finally does decide to cross over!

Here are some of Grandma's current thoughts on this issue, as she recently "korasponded" them to me:

"As for funeral plans for myself, I've had a lot of them. By now, I've crossed off three pages of potential pall bearers because they've all died off. I'm on my third page for them. Now when I see the ones currently slated for the job, I make it a point to ask them, 'How are you today?'" she laughs.

They will typically respond, "Well, how am I supposed to be?"

"Well, I just put you down as a pall bearer and I gotta keep you healthy!" Grandma emphasized.

Grandma has already looked at caskets and various color schemes therein. She has her singers lined up, although one of those ladies has already died.

"Hated that," sighed Grandma, "as she was supposed to play the organ at my funeral, too. Now I have to find a new one, so I better get busy on that."

As for her obituary, she says she'll just leave that up to her son Blaine.

What about food at the funeral?

"Well, of course! I've already planned the post-burial dinner! However, I have to keep changing that, too, as the servers and cooks I have selected are dying off on me, too"

What's a 106-year-old woman to do? Live forever, I suppose!

CONTINUALLY PRAISE THE YOUNGER GENERATIONS

Grandma is never at a loss for encouraging words when it comes to her great grandkids....all nine of them. "I always tell them that they are smart kids, nice kids, and full of potential. You have to get those ideas engrained in their minds while they are still young yet," Grandma reminds us. "If they understand the positive things about themselves and truly believe them, success in life will just naturally follow."

Appreciate Your Body, Even When You Are in Your 80s

One hot, summer day over 20 years ago, Grandma came to Kansas City to spend some time with my parents. One afternoon, she came up to my room and sat down beside me on the bed to engage in conversation and catch up on all of the exciting things in my life. The dialogue was going well when suddenly, there was an unexpected pause. Grandma looked down at her legs and then over at my legs, and proudly commented, "Will you look at that? My legs look better than yours! How'd that happen?" (I have not stopped running since!)

How to Act Like an Old Lady

If you are a woman reading this, let's face it! We sometimes dread those later years of our lives in terms of how they might affect us both physically and mentally. Who wants to grow old and decrepit, right? There seems to be a consistent and growing trend in eating healthier, exercising more, and maintaining a positive attitude. Those are all great indicators that as we glide into the sunset of our lives that the transition will most likely be seamless and pleasant. However, I often wonder why we seem to stress ourselves out with the age thing. After all, our bodies are not meant to last forever. In observing Grandma over the years, I have found that the best way to keep the clock of time from creeping up on you rests in the daily use of laughter and good humor, complemented by a clear presence of mind.

At age 47, I sometimes feel as if I am gearing up for the senior citizen lifestyle. After all, there are some days when my mailbox is holding a "Come Visit Our New Senior Care Facility" invitation with my name in bold letters on the front. I frequently ask myself just how 47 became the new 87, and I cannot figure it all out.

The reason for my confusion rests mainly in the abiding presence of Grandma, who, on her next birthday in 2012, will blow out 107 candles. One could reasonably assume she is resting comfortably in a secluded nursing home, wheel-chair bound, and staring blankly at a fuzzy television set. Amidst mental confusion, she might ask a nursing attendant if Truman won or if she could give the gal a dime to go get a loaf of bread. However, this 106-year-old woman is here to show how 106 is the new 56!

If you have ever wondered exactly how to act like an old lady, or just an older person for that matter, then take some unsolicited advice from Grandma. You just might set yourself apart from the thundering herd in doing so.

1. At your 100th birthday party, be sure to come out in a bathrobe in front of everyone and start to do a striptease. Sexily sway your hips back and forth and slowly reveal your stunning 40-year-old bathing suit. Let the act immediately stop there, grab a Margarita, and head for the nearest hot tub.

2. When you get your photo taken in honor of your 100th birthday, examine the proofs and tell the photographer that you think your face looks too wrinkled. When the photographer assures you that he can airbrush those out for just $100.00 more, tell the photographer to just photograph you from a little further away for free. Thus, the wrinkles are far less visible, and you have saved yourself $100.00!

3. When you are 103 years of age and on vacation in Colorado, take a spin on a motorcycle. When someone offers you assistance on getting on the bike, slap his hand and proclaim, "I can do this myself!"

4. When you catch your 45-year-old granddaughter working on the computer, ask her about those Internet porn sites. Then see how you respond when she says, "Gee, Grandma....looks like I have found your profile here!"

5.   When you are on a Caribbean cruise to celebrate yet ANOTHER birthday, grab your granddaughter's new husband and take him up to the topless deck. After all, you want to see if anything has changed from that standpoint since the early 1900s!

6.   When it is time to go out to dinner, head to the nearest buffet-style restaurant. Rush immediately to the buffet to see if the food is anything to your liking. Sample a few things here and there by simply reaching into the dishes with your hands. After several samples and several long minutes, decide you would be better served if you headed across the street to McDonald's, where the coffee is free for seniors!

7.   When the nation elects a new President, get nervous, call your daughter-in-law, and lament relentlessly about how worried you are about your financial future. After all, at 103, the current economy could profoundly affect your retirement plans!

8.   Ask your grandkids if you are in their wills!

9.   Gross out the great-grandkids who reach into your purse for a mint and find two baggies side-by-side. Tell them one bag holds your leftovers from that meal at McDonald's and that the other baggie holds your stool sample for your doctor. The mints will remain in your purse untouched from there on out.

10. At age 102, experience a phenomenon that would appall most women: start menstruating again. "I have seen this in some women her age," noted her doctor. To which I wanted to reply, "Exactly how many women her age have you seen?" Grandma was just upset as she had to go buy "those dang maxi pads" again.

11. Decide that, at 105 years of age, you want to pack up and move....start over, as you are getting rather bored in your current location.

These are just a few handy reminders of how to act like an "old woman." (Or man; just skip #10 in that case, please!)

THE WEATHER WAS COLD. THE FORECAST WAS CHALLENGING. THE DRIVE WAS LONG. THE PATIENCE WAS THIN.

In late 2008, Grandma, almost 104, left her small Midwestern town in search of warmer climates for the holidays. Up by 4 a.m. this particular morning, there was no time for her usual free coffee at her local McDonald's. She had to hit the road for the four hour drive to the nearest international airport. A "younger" friend, someone in her late 60s, was chaperoning Grandma to the airport. Once there and checked in, it was all up to Grandma to get to her southern destination.

When she boarded her flight, her first order of business was most likely chatting up the flight attendants and attempting to advise the pilots as to a more efficient flight pattern to their destination. She probably requested additional packets of the in-flight peanuts, which she would place in her antiquated handbag and re-gift later in the week to her wide-eyed great-grandkids.

There may have been an in-flight movie. Grandma's hearing was not what it used to be. Even if she used those complimentary ear buds, chances are, the volume was turned up so high that, while Grandma still couldn't hear most of the dialogue, someone three rows back did.

She would then peruse an in-flight magazine. After three minutes of engaged reading, she'd turn to her fellow passenger and strike up a conversation. "My name is Kora...with a K," as she is fond of saying. "I am 104 years old. I am going to see my son for Christmas." Once the listener began to respond, within seconds, Grandma was snoring, head drooping to one side until subtle turbulence knocked her out of her light trance.

She would fidget a bit in her seat, worry that she was running late, and question everyone in sight, "Why can't this dang plane go any faster?" as she nervously looked out the window to see if they had moved any closer to their intended destination. Christmas was six days away, yet she was concerned she would be late.

Grandma has a unique history of flying around the world in her lifetime. She once flew on the famed Concord from England to the United States, not only to experience how quickly it actually did soar, but to see if, in that shortened time across the pond, her in-flight meal could be served AND consumed before they landed.

Grandma's travels have taken her all over Europe, Africa, Russia, the Mediterranean, and more. She has never been one to let life pass her by. While enjoying one excursion, she will be brilliantly planning the next one.

She has no fear of "expiring" any time soon. Her anticipated "expiration date" will be in the month of August, year yet to be determined. Why August? Well, the answer to that is simple. It is the most convenient month for most people in her family to attend a funeral.

"Mom," her youngest son has emphasized over the years, "whenever you plan to die, make sure it is in August, as I have the most free time in that month. Any other time would simply be inconvenient."

True to her son, after all of these years, Grandma has yet to inconvenience him. Every summer, she will attempt to reorganize any potential funeral plans, and when the month of August comes and goes without incident, she is confident she has yet another year to make plans, to travel, and to have fun. She has spent countless hours re-configuring her pending funeral arrangements. Her biggest upset was this past summer.

"I just spent two weeks with the little gal who was to play the organ at my funeral," noted Grandma, "and then she had to up and die on me a week later." Undaunted, Grandma furiously went to work to make other arrangements. With Grandma still kicking about, understudies are necessary for upcoming roles in her funeral.

"When you live to be as old as I am," Grandma explains, "not only have your friends died, but your friends kids begin to die." As such, plans for the future constantly have to be modified. Funeral eulogies are continually updated as Grandma's life moves forward. Even all of the pall bearers she originally assigned to the task at least two decades ago have passed on.

I suspect, however, that once Grandma does make her final flight plans, they will be well attended, and she will be soaring to that grand vacation spot in the sky. We just have to make sure there are plenty of packets of peanuts along the way!

As for her famous tag line of, "It's Kora...with a K," Grandma changed her name around the age of 15 when a group of her friends decided, for a lark, to change the spelling of their first names by one letter. Cora chose Kora. Another gal, named Alma, went to Almah. While the other gals never formally maintained these changes, Grandma did. "I never did like Cora with a C," she snipped. "The day I forget my own name, however, is the day it's over for me," she says.

"I have enough trouble remembering other people's names."

After a brief pause, she laughs, "At least I can still eat. As long as I am eating, consider me to be well. If you call me one day and I indicate I have no appetite, that's when I want you to know the end is near!"

KORA... THIRD FROM LEFT, CIRCA 1925

THE SECRET TO HAPPINESS IN LIFE

Are you one of those individuals who is constantly in search of happiness, but you struggle to find it? Do you know why? It's because it is right under your nose...within your heart. You have to look there first; otherwise, you will never find it. It will always remain elusive, and you will just wear yourself out pursuing it.

I should have listened to Grandma years ago. She always told me to simply pursue the things in life that would make me happy. While I did that personally, I am really just beginning to do that professionally. As selfish as it sounds, happiness begins within ourselves, and if we can't find it there, we won't find it anywhere. That is why I decided to write this book. It is what makes me genuinely happy. It is my mission to share her wit and wisdom with the world. Besides, the Universe made me do it!

"IT'S EITHER IN YA OR IT'S NOT IN YA."

Grandma has always been like my own personal GPS. She has a very distinct way of knowing whether I should pursue something or not. She hones in on her own personal passions and endeavors in much the same way...always has. Some of us call it instinct. Some of us call it a feeling our in gut. Whatever the case, when you know, you just know. Don't second guess anything. That little voice inside your head (and if there are more than one, that might be an issue for you!) is trying to tell you something, so listen up!

For instance, I hate to cook. I have never loved anything about food that way. For me, the kitchen has simply been a passage way from the garage to the living room. Nothing more. Nothing less. I leave the task of cooking to the experts. Even my own three boys were relieved back in early 2000 when I relinquished the cooking duties to my husband. "Thanks, Mom," they all said, with more relief in their voices than I actually hoped to hear!

At any rate, Grandma made several attempts to put the kitchen in me over the years, but to no avail. I simply had no interest in pots, pans, recipes, and the like, much less entertaining. I am hardly like Grandma in that regard.

About the time I turned 16 years of age, Grandma simply told me after yet another experiment in the kitchen failed, "Well, if it's not in ya, it's not in ya. No amount of practicing will overcome that." And she proceeded to take off her apron, gently fold it, and put it in the drawer. Like that. Buried. I would never be a cook in her eyes....and the focal point of her life has always been about food. I kind of feel like I failed her in that regard, but what could I do? I had no interest in it. I still don't. So...that was that. She never forced the issue again. She knew.

As with anything in life, if you don't feel it in you to do it, if it does not inspire you, don't force it. It will never happen under such conditions, and if it does, it will probably just crash and burn....much like that casserole did that I was attempting to make back in 1979. Trust me. You don't want me in the kitchen. Betty Crocker does not have me on speed dial, and Rachel Ray would only find comic relief in my antics. Heck! I think I have even screwed up take out on occasion! The only thing I should do with food is eat it, but only in moderation. Grandma has always stressed that! "Eat what you want, but in moderation only. You don't want go get fat now, do you?"

WATER, WATER EVERYWHERE!

You had to have been there to fully appreciate this little gem, but I have to pass it along. Grandma is a big consumer of water. She knows its health benefits, and she has always pointed her finger in my direction to remind me to drink plenty of it. I do. I love it, actually, which is why I take many trips to the bathroom each day.

One sunny Saturday afternoon in January of 2009, my husband and I had the pleasure of spending time with Grandma on one of her visits to Kansas City. As we were out driving around, Grandma got a hankering for a cheeseburger, so we stopped in at her favorite spot – McDonald's! She has been a customer for life and should actually be the face of the company. If someone can eat McDonald's for decades on end and is still thriving at 106, that bears some research, right?

After we had eaten our little meal in the restaurant, which, by the way, was crowded with families that particular afternoon, Grandma made sure to refill her water cup and carry it with her as we walked towards the door to go to the car.

As she was walking through the restaurant, she proudly proclaimed (and loudly, too, I might add!), "Ahh...that sure tastes good. You have to drink water and plenty of it!" A few onlookers watched her stroll on by, as she does garner a lot of attention wherever she goes these days. After a brief pause, she then added in decibels higher than normal, "Drinking water makes for good bowel movements, did you know that? I love a good bowel movement."

I tried not to laugh or look at others around me who heard this grand proclamation, but nearly everyone in the place had. I was equal parts mortified and proud. Sure, what she said was embarrassing, but more to the point, she spoke her mind and enjoyed the results. She didn't say anything negative, nor did she slur someone's name. She just made a statement of fact....just a bit too loud for my tastes, however.

Now, I don't know if anyone in McDonald's that day will remember the blue-haired gal that walked among them talking about her bowel activities, but if just one person drank more water that day, then Grandma did her job.

SPEAKING OF BOWEL MOVEMENTS...
"ONE SQUARE!"

I learned the basic mechanics of pre-Depression indoor plumbing systems at a relatively early age. When I was a young girl, it was not unusual for me to use the bathroom and essentially go through a whole roll of toilet paper in one sitting. I wanted to make sure I was completely clean, you see, and I will note that my three boys are sometimes guilty of this same behavior today.

My overuse of toilet paper always created a "situation" when I was at Grandma's house. The plumbing in her home was not as capable of successfully flushing large quantities as the plumbing to which I had grown accustomed in my parents' house. Frequently, in my efforts to make sure I was fully cleaned after each trip to the bathroom, my over-indulgence of the sanitary supplies would create a back log in the plumbing. Yep! The toilet in Grandma's house would become clogged.

Boy, oh boy! Did that ever upset Grandma! The first few times, she simply overlooked it, but after I had forced her to wield the plunger one too many times, she immediately enforced a new rule: One square for pee; two squares for poop.

What? Are you kidding me? I can never get myself clean with such a small ration. Surely she must be kidding. Nope! In fact, on one occasion, she actually stood outside the bathroom door while I was on the other side of it taking care of business, and when I had completed the task at hand, she simply asked me, "Shall I slip one or two squares under the door?"

Sometimes, during the one week each summer I would stay at Grandma's house, I would self-inflict constipation, as I knew I could not successfully wipe myself with just two squares. Too bad she did not have a bidet! Then again, that would have resulted in overuse of water! Grandma has always been the consummate saver!

Interestingly enough, every time I use the bathroom today, I still hear that voice in my head, "One square! One square!" Thank goodness I have the kind of toilets in my home that can flush a dozen golf balls at once!

GRANDMA KORA, IN THE INFAMOUS "ONE SQUARE, TWO SQUARE" BATHROOM IN THE 1950S...BEFORE MY TIME...BUT MY TIME WAS COMING!

TYPICAL GRANDMA

Grandma has always loved to write notes and letters to reveal to the recipients the little bits and pieces of her day. Nothing was too small to mention. Everything bore significance. Just take a peek at this pearl of wisdom I found in my belongings. At the time, I was living in Dallas, Texas, pursuing post-collegiate studies in the paralegal field.

April 21, 1990:

Dear Ann:

Hi! Just back from breakfast at McDonald's. Beautiful day out – but was terribly foggy when we went out - - could only see about a block. Went to the horse races Wed. at Grand Island, Neb. and had fun. Got to be in the club room and had a lovely buffet at noon in there also. En route home, ate at the Golden Corral in Hastings, Neb. Tuesday the other bank in town entertains the "First Ladies" at a luncheon at the Elks Club, and the next morn, my bank is giving us a free movie of "Miss Daisy" and doughnuts and coffee before the show in the lobby. More fun with these 2 banks vying against each other. Of course, you have to have so much money in each bank before you are a member of this club.

How's school? Know it is hard but am sure you can make it. What did you think of the articles I sent in regards to this type of work? Sounded good, eh?

Started my Dr. Atkins diet yesterday for 2 weeks!

Love,

Grma H.

Grandma was always starting some diet or another, but she always prefaced it with this: "I'm going to start my diet on Monday!" I don't think Monday ever really came!

I'M SORRY, GRANDMA, BUT I DISOBEYED YOU!

As I was rummaging through old letters from Grandma, I came across this one in particular. Again, it gives testament to what matters most to her and as to how she takes control of things in life, dispensing advice, being her own advocate, and clearly making decisions. When you get to the end of the letter, you will discover just how I disobeyed her. To clarify a few things, during this time, I was married to a man to whom I never should have gotten married. Let's just say drugs and abuse were involved, and not on my part. Grandma was so concerned about me at that time, and she was always one of the first to render her opinion and steer me in the right direction. Everyone needs Grandma Kora or someone like her to guide them!

(This one particular letter was written on Princess Cruises stationery. One of the perks of going on cruises: free note paper to take home!)

February 23, 1991:

Dear Ann,

Well, I was watching the KU-Oklahoma game on TV, but it makes me so nervous, so I just better write you a letter, probably my last until I come down to visit.

I guess, as it stands now, Steven will drive to Salina, where he will leave his car at Bob's. But he can't leave much before 4 p.m., so that means eating late in Salina. I was hoping he could leave earlier and we could drive as far as Shorty's, but I guess he can't. So, we'll try and get a really early morning start on Saturday to be there...sometime late in the P.M. I hope Steven gets the instructions as to how to get there, so that doesn't take us so long.

Ann, I have a couple ideas for you, and neither may work, but just a thought. Why don't you ask Joe if he would move out for a trial separation and tell him if he would do that, Steven could help him move. Do you think he would do this? Then another idea. Do you know the landlord of the apartments very well? I thought you might ask her if she has any cheap empty apartments and that is if you don't have a lease on yours where you are now, then you could rent the new one, and when Joe was at work, you could move in, hopefully while we are in Dallas. If no lease and they have an empty apartment, that would be a slick idea. If nothing else, you're just going to have to get an eviction notice out on him to get him out. Aren't you working for a lawyer? Also, do you know the name of the company he is working for, and the address? One could always garnish his wages for what he owes one. Or, if he would only be willing to give you his key to the apartment so he couldn't take things out.

I had a lovely birthday, 4 of us out to eat at McDonald's and gave me a cute balloon that said, "Roses are red, violets are blue, I'm laughing like hell because I'm younger than you!" Then in the evening, Lil took 3 of us to dinner at Hays and we came back here and played a little bridge, then watched the USA pageant and Kansas won! This morn I was out for breakfast — at McDonald's — and tonight going to a buffet at the Elks for the Russell Arts Council. I certainly do thank you for the certificate for McDonald's - wonderful idea, but you shouldn't have spent so much. Blaine and Judy sent me a gorgeous bouquet, and I'm going to take it to church tomorrow.

My shoulder is better and a pic this morning said it was plenty healed, but my hand is horrible. I just can't bend it at all, and it throbs at all times. Darvon or pills don't seem to faze it. During the night last night, I thought I was getting a blood clot again, as I had these shooting pains up my leg, but went to the doc this morning and he said he didn't think so and gave me some medicine to thin my blood, said it was too thick.

Well, nothing more to add, I guess, so may take time out to go down to mail it. All my love and keep your chin up. Tear up this letter.

Grdma H.

"EVERYTHING HAPPENS FOR A REASON."

Grandma's favorite philosophy in life: Everything happens for a reason. I know some people take issue with this. Some believe in fate, divine intervention, whatever you want to call it. Others just laugh it off as coincidence. I prefer to side with Grandma on this issue, and I'm not apologizing for it, either.

In September 1997, I found out I was pregnant with my third child. I had just finished graduate school and was contemplating re-entering the work force. I also had two other children, ages two and one, so the thought of having another child terrified me.

I called my husband at work first and warned him to sit down before I relayed the news to him. After all, we were a struggling young family with two little ones. How could we possibly afford another one?

I made the usual round of calls to other family members but saved the call to Grandma for last. When she answered the phone and I told her the news, her response was matter-of-fact, and one that I will never forget:

"Ann, I have always told you that everything happens in life for a reason. If you are driving down the road and the light turns red when you want it to remain green, it turned red for a reason. Perhaps God was sparing you from an accident down the road. Never get upset for the way things happen in life, as there is always a reason for the manner in which they happen."

I remember being near tears as I was talking about this third pregnancy, but she would have none of it.

"Ann, there's a reason this baby is supposed to be born. You may not know it next year, you may not know it for ten years, but there is a reason. Now get over it and be glad."

As I look at my son now, that "baby for a reason," who will turn 13 on June 22, 2011, I know beyond a shadow of a doubt that Grandma was right. It was as if an angel was speaking through her.

Noah Spencer Butenas was born on June 22, 1998. That was the very day on which Grandma gave birth to her two boys – my dad, L.A. in 1933 and my Uncle Blaine in 1935. Noah evidently decided that June 22nd was a good day. Here's where it gets eerie, however.

Now that Noah is coming into his own, I see so much evidence of the spirit of my dad in him. I sometimes feel as if Noah is my dad, coming back to take care of me. He is so much like my father, it's difficult not to believe it. My dad passed away five years and 19 days before Noah was born. I do not find it a coincidence that Noah came into this world on June 22nd. I also do not find it a coincidence that Noah aspires to be a physician. My dad and my uncle both pursued careers as doctors.

Noah also bears a remarkable heart of service and even at his young age, has won two awards from two different schools he has attended for the manner in which he exemplifies the virtues of respect, responsibility, honesty, self-discipline, compassion, courage, and perseverance. Those words could easily define my dad.

Part of Noah's plan in life is to become an eye doctor. He has actually calculated that, if all things go according to schedule, he will commence medical school in this regard in the year 2020. (Again, I don't believe this a coincidence!)

Unique to Noah is his recent commitment to his faith and to church, something that was very important to my dad. Noah has a heart of service and one day hopes to take his financial earnings as an eye doctor and create a non-profit called "Noah's Ark." He wants to take food, supplies, and medical services to those in need, whether across the US or throughout the world. At 13, he is not sure how he will accomplish this, but he just knows he will. My dad frequently went to the inner city when he was alive and gave free physicals to the homeless at a place in Kansas City called the City Union Mission.

Born for a reason? You already know my answer to that one, and Grandma's response as well. I will leave your opinion up to you, but it's difficult to not see the obvious in this one. I believe Noah is picking up where my dad left off.

I also know that my two older sons have an express purpose in life, as well. Both are intelligent, independent thinkers and are highly ambitious. Both have talent beyond the very scope of my own, and I know that all three of my sons will grow up to be fine young men, bearing a significant reflection on Grandma's passion for service, hard-work, education, determination, and grace. I am so grateful that she has been able to see them grow up thus far, something my dad never had the opportunity to do. I remember my dad telling my mom during his final days that one of his regrets would be that he would never live to see grandkids. I know he has seen them from above, and I am confident his spirit lives on in Noah, as when Noah is with me, I feel my dad's presence. That's my story and I'm sticking with it.

"This is Your Stop, Mom! Gotta Go!"

Remember that 70-mile punishment story? Life sometimes has a way of coming back to sting you in the hindquarters if you're not careful. This is a story that was relayed to me by my mom and brother a short time ago. I had no knowledge of this previously, but find it quite amusing.

As the story goes, my uncle Blaine was driving Grandma to the Denver airport after a family vacation in the mountains. He was presumably going at his usual frenetic pace with his hair on fire to get to the terminal on time. He realized that he was cutting it short if he wanted to get Grandma to her plane, return the rental car, and get to his gate all within a relatively short amount of time.

As he was cruising down the highway, he came upon an unexpected road block that really threw a wrench in his plans. Time was not on his side right now. Road crews and equipment trucks had brought the traffic to a standstill. If he did not do something, everyone would miss their flights.

He breathlessly managed to get to the rental car facility, but knew he had would never get Grandma to her flight on time if he attempted to take her from there. As such, he inquired of an employee in the place if she would be so kind as to take Grandma for him. As I understand it, the employee, recognizing my uncle's predicament, volunteered to do this anyway. So, Uncle Blaine left Grandma at the rental car place, with her luggage beside her on the curb and bid her farewell, entrusting a stranger to get Grandma to her plane on time. However, as far as Grandma is concerned, she never knows a stranger, so it really didn't matter. She made it to the terminal on time and all was well. That's customer service, though, isn't it?

ESSENCE OF GIVING

While rummaging through Grandma's old recipe box, I came across this old newspaper clipping. Grandma loved to cook, entertain, and feed others, but I believe what she served best was her timeless wisdom.

"Perhaps the young woman from the 'old school' of kindness should remember the old adage, 'He who gives from a sense of duty gives nothing but worthless gold.'"

Food for thought...

THERE'S NO SUCH THING AS A CHOCOLATE CHIP!

I learned from an early age that there is no such thing as a chocolate chip cookie, chocolate chip ice cream, or chocolate chip pie. Not in the Hollinger household, that is! Grandma was an amazing cook and an equally-impressive baker. Among her favorite things to create were chip chocolate cookies and chip chocolate pie. The chip ALWAYS came before the chocolate! If you have a recipe for chocolate chip cookies or chocolate chip pie, it is not Grandma's!

Here are two of her famous recipes! As you know, I am neither a cook nor a baker, so don't ask me to interpret anything here! These are "as is" from her recipe file.

Chip Chocolate Cookies

1 cup Crisco

1 cup white sugar

1 cup brown sugar (cream)

2 eggs

2 cups flour

½ t. salt

1 t. soda

1 t. vanilla

1 cup nuts

1 pkg. Bakers Sweet choc chips

Bake at 375 degrees for ten minutes. Enjoy!

Chip Chocolate Pie

32 large marshmallows

1 cup milk

(Cook over low heat until marshmallows are melted. Cool
thoroughly.)

Add:

1 cup cream, whipped

2 squares regular baking chocolate cut into pieces (not too fine)

½ cup nuts

Add a dash of vanilla and a speck of salt

Put into pie shell and chill

NEW YORK, NEW YORK!

Grandma's older sister, Sadie Lou Lindenmeyer Told, left the sleepy town of Russell, Kansas, when she was barely 21 years old. She met a man named William Henry Told and began an amazing life with him in Palm Beach, Florida. That marriage produced one son, William "Billy" Henry Told, Jr., a wonderful man with whom I have grown close over the years. He is my dad's cousin, therefore my first cousin, once removed, but more like a dear uncle to me. His life story and that of his parents should be captured in a book. However, for the purposes of this book, Billy has shared some interesting stories and anecdotes about my grandma that made me laugh and smile when I heard them. He showed me my grandmother in a light I had never before seen.

When Billy took a job with a major bank in New York City in the 1950s, Grandma made sure to visit him there, check out the night life, and basically just make her general presence known. The Big Apple had no idea what was in store for it!

According to Billy, Grandma pretty much had the place figured out before she even got there. She knew where all the great restaurants were and made reservations to go there. She also picked out some of the hottest night clubs for dancing and carrying on in the night hours. To hear Billy tell it, it was as if Grandma had been born and raised in that city. She had no fear and pursued that which interested her. It didn't matter what other people thought. She was there to have fun, and fun she had!

On one particular weekend afternoon, Grandma, Billy, and some of the gang (probably my uncle Blaine and a few friends of Billy's, from what I recall), headed over to Coney Island to check out the excitement. No fear of heights, twists, turns, or increased velocity, Grandma enthusiastically jumped on a ride similar to a whirl-a-gig. It was a ride that spun around in circles while moving up and down. Grandma just hooted and hollered the whole time, as if nothing else in time and space existed. She was simply having a blast, indulging her inner child, and she didn't care who heard her or who saw her. She was in heaven!

After Grandma enjoyed the ride several times, the operator of the whirl-a-gig invited her to continue riding for free for the rest of the day. No tickets required.

"That's the best advertisement I've had in a long time for this thing!" he laughed.

SERIOUSLY? A DRESS ON A MOUNTAIN TOP? DEFINITELY NOT
CASUAL FRIDAY IN THE ROCKIES BACK IN 1965! GRANDMA
KORA HAS ALWAYS BEEN FASHIONABLE! THAT'S ME, BY THE
WAY, THE LITTLE CUTIE STANDING IN FRONT OF GRANDPA!
MY MOM AND OLDER BROTHER ARE ALSO PICTURED HERE.

FROM THE PAGES OF THE RUSSELL RECORD

Whenever something special or significant happened in our lives, Grandma would be sure to have it written up in her hometown paper, the Russell Record. Heck! Even if I just went and visited her for a week in the summer, she would do a blurb about it, focusing on what we did and on what we ate that week, and then have it printed in the paper. I always felt like such a celebrity in that regard.

Here is a newspaper clipping from the Russell Record that started it all, dated March 28, 1927:

The marriage of Miss Cora Marie Lindenmeyer, daughter of Mr. and Mrs. H.A. Lindenmeyer, and Mr. Lloyd L. Hollinger, son of Mr. and Mrs. A.C. Hollinger, was solemnized this morning at 10 o'clock at the Lindenmeyer home. Only the immediate families of the couple were present. Following the ceremony, luncheon was served. Mr. and Mrs. Hollinger will make their home in Ponca City, Oklahoma, where the groom has accepted a position in George Hume's drug store.

Mrs. Hollinger has been employed as stenographer to Attorney J.E. Driscoll for the past three years since the completion of her business course in Salina. Mr. Hollinger is a graduate pharmacist of the Kansas City Pharmaceutical College and has been employed in Turner's Drug Store.

Miss Lois Beardsley played and sang, "All for You" and "I Love You Truly." The bride's dress was of navy blue georgette trimmed in red and she wore a corsage of American beauty rose buds.

Mr. and Mrs. Hollinger will leave today or tomorrow for their new home going by way of Manhattan, Topeka, and Kansas City where they will visit friends this week. Their many friends here join in extending congratulations.

Believe it or not, this was actually front page news! No surprise there! The folks at the newspaper knew they were on to something with Grandma!

NEVER ARGUE WITH A 105-YEAR-OLD WOMAN ABOUT WHO IS THE BOSS!

In April of 2010, I drove out to Russell to visit Grandma. When I was younger, I enjoyed visiting her for the good eats I'd be assured. Now that I am older, I prefer to load up on her infectious wit, wisdom, and passion for life.

During the course of our conversation, I had the opportunity to ask her the most compelling of all questions, and I wanted to find out her answer to this question because my husband was in the room and I felt, knowing how my grandma thinks, her response would be of great benefit to him. So, I proceeded with the inquiry.

"Grandma," I began. "What makes for a successful marriage?"

Without missing a beat, she replied, looking first at me and then darting a troubled glance at my husband. "Why? Are you having trouble?"

I laugh and say, "No, not at all. I just want to know how you and Grandpa kept the romantic and loving fires burning for over 50 years."

With an understanding nod, Grandma tells me, "That's easy. Be the boss!"

I then shot a knowing glance to my husband, making sure he caught that sentiment. He did, but for some reason, did not find the inherent humor in it as I did.

I turn back to my grandma and asked her to elaborate.

"When I say you should be the boss, I mean you, as the woman, should take care of all of the household things, the bills, the finances, the kids, and all of the major decisions. Just let the man take care of whatever is left in the garage. Let him worry about the car and the trash."

I am still enamored with her quick sentiment: Be the boss! I love it! Visions of me dictating the who, the what, the where, and the when dance in my mind. Then my husband of nearly 17 years brings me back to earth and tells me, "Ann, you do all of that already. You trained me well."

THE DOG THAT BIT ME! (AND THE HAIR OF GRANDMA'S THAT I GOT INTO!)

It was the summer of 1972. It was a very hot and humid afternoon in the thriving metropolis of Russell, Kansas...population in the low thousands or so! Grandma had commenced her weekly bridge game on this particular day, so I was politely encouraged to leave the house for a few hours and explore around the neighborhood, which I happily did. I had no interest in hanging out with a bunch of old people playing cards and carrying on. Grandma got into that game like an NFL coach gets fired up for the Super Bowl game. Unbelievable.

As I hopped on my bike and made my way around the neighborhood, I came upon a cute little dog. Unable to resist his anticipated loving affections, I got off the bike, laid it on the ground, and walked up to the dog, hand outstretched and saying something like, "Hey, little puppy. How are you today?"

Just as I got within one or two inches of this adorable creature, the beast within him reared its ugly head and he lunged at my face, taking a big bite into my upper lip. I panicked. Within seconds, I felt a cold sensation running over my mouth and down my chin, onto my shirt. I placed my hand to my mouth and then brought that hand into view. I screamed bloody murder! My hand was covered in grossness! I screamed. I cried. I left my bicycle on the ground and ran as fast as I could back to Grandma's house.

Unfortunately, Grandpa was not at home at the time, leaving me to deal with the unpleasant scenario that I was certain would soon unfold. You see, interrupting Grandma's bridge game was akin to laughing out loud in church. It was a sacred time. Not to be disturbed. As I approached her driveway, my shirt now stained with blood and my face presumably looking like I'd been in a fight, I stopped in my tracks and began to wonder exactly how I would handle this.

"Maybe I can just sneak inside and grab some towels and take care of this myself," I mused.

As the blood continued to ooze from the gaping hole (Well, to me it was a gaping hole. I was nine and in my mind I was probably going to bleed out right there on the driveway!)

I was smart enough to know that this particular wound was going to require medical assistance, so I did what I felt was most appropriate at the time, given the dire circumstances. I stood right outside the screen door on the side of her house and screamed at the top of my lungs.

Within seconds, Grandma rushed to the door, several cards still in her hand, and she gave me a rather horrified look. At first, I wasn't sure if she was horrified by my appearance or if she was horrified that she was about to win a game but was so rudely interrupted.

In her usual fashion, annoyed but remaining the dutiful Grandma, she quickly called off the game and wiped me up a bit. We got in the car and headed over to the emergency room to get me fixed up.

Later in the evening, as we sat around in her den watching TV, Grandpa snoozing on one end of the divan and myself holding a cold pack to my upper lip on the other, I gazed over at my grandma who, by this time, was deeply engrossed in one of those nightly game shows on TV. I felt badly that I had disturbed her bridge game, but I felt grateful that she took care of me that day.

The only thing she told me before I went to bed that evening was this:

"Don't ever bend down to pet a strange dog again, you hear me?" Then after a brief pause, she added, "At least not on bridge day."

That's all I needed to hear. Her sense of humor still intact, I knew that I had really done no wrong. I still have a slight scar from my battle with the Beagle. Every time I look at it, it takes me back to that hot and humid afternoon in the summer of 1972 in Russell, Kansas. I don't think of the dog when I see it. I think of a Grandmother's love....for me, and, yes...for the game of bridge! Tough call, but she obviously made the right choice that day!

A LOVING TRIBUTE TO A WONDERFUL ORGANIST

Monday the 26ᵗʰ 1979

Dear One and All:

Am carbon copying this as want to send a copy to L.A., Blaine, Sadie, and Sarah. All about our church service yesterday morning. Blaine called this morn – before 8, and could have told him, but forgot. Anyway, yesterday we dedicated our new organ and our new robes and for the organ part, had a guest organist, and boy was she good – showed me up! Also, it was our minister's birthday and I knew about this - - that in the middle of the service, our choir director came forward with a small cake, with one candle on it, and Ruth hit the chord and everyone sang "Happy Birthday."

Then, Norma Jean (choir dir.) said a few words about how much they appreciated him, and then she said, "Kora, will you come up here?" I was already nervous, as Ruth and I played a piano and organ prelude and offertory and I did other parts of the service. Well, I was so shocked, and I went up, and she read to the congregation the poetry which I will copy below, which her mother had made up, and I stood there and cried and Norma Jean said she didn't or couldn't look at me, or she would, too.

And then the whole church gave me a gift - - it was a charm for my bracelet...an organ with a stool - - can you imagine that? I shall always cherish that. Well, I've never been so surprised. Will copy verses below. Mary and Harold Mc. Came up for it, and they ate dinner here at the house with us before going home. It was a beautiful service. Wish you all could have been here.

Not much else news. Blaine called as they plan to leave for Rome around April 26th, and I guess we will go down and stay with the kids and am glad it isn't towards latter part of May, as I'm sure that is when Steve's graduation is, and we had told them we couldn't come then, if it was. They will be gone about 2 weeks, I guess...will travel a little. They're supposed to start their house April 1st, too.

Lloyd had gone up to the hospital to give sample of urine. It had been 7 weeks I guess since he was up. Plan to go to Hays tomorrow, I think.

Can't think of anything else, so want to get this off in the mail. I go to a luncheon and bridge today noon. Susan, you might show your folks the poetry, and Sadie, you might send to Billy, and Sarah to Minor. She usually sends my letter and then I don't write him, so thanks.

Love, Mother

Tribute to Our Organist--Kora
Since this is a very special day
For our church and congregation
A happy occasion all can share
With grateful enjoyment and recognition.

On this day we realize
We have a special friend
Who is faithful in her duty.
For her faithfulness we commend.

These words were written to confess
How neglectful we have been
To thank you for your helpfulness
Our apologies we extend.

For many years you've played for us
I expect two score and more
Always faithful - - always willing
Playing the music we adore

An organ is just an instrument
Setting there all alone
Until someone play it
Its usefulness is forlorn.

We didn't mean to be neglectful
Nor selfish, but you see
We just took Kora for granted
On the organ we knew she'd be.

The organ music is so inspiring
And helps the service, true
The tone of every note that's played
Is an accomplishment of you.

And when it comes to organists
Your presence we can trust
So now we hope you realize
How much you mean to us.

(Written by Inez Tomlin)

ON BEING STRICT WITH THE KIDS

Grandma will be the first to admit that she ruled her boys with a pretty heavy hand, not so much in terms of physical punishment, but in terms of expectations. Yes, she did keep a measuring stick just above the kitchen door, and, on more than one occasion, had to use it on the boys, but those lessons learned were few and far between.

No, greater still was how she stressed her expectations of them. Grandpa was fully behind her in this endeavor, but, once again, the ever out-spoken Kora Hollinger most decidedly ruled the roost.

However, the manner in which she raised her kids will elicit tears from her today when she reflects upon those early years.

"Yes, I was a strict mom," she will admit, tears welling in her eyes. However, a kind word spoken in reflection by my father on the day he graduated from medical school assuaged her feelings immensely in this regard.

After the pomp and circumstance of the ceremonies that day back in 1960, Grandma was reduced to tears, not only because of the joy she felt in seeing her oldest boy accept his medical degree, but also because of her suppressed feelings of guilt over the disciplined manner in which she raised her boys.

When my dad caught her crying and she told him her true feelings, he simply said, "But, Mom, maybe Blaine and I wouldn't be today who we are...two doctors...if you hadn't been so strict with us." (At this time, my uncle Blaine was still in medical school and would graduate two years later, giving Grandma yet another opportunity to express her guilt!)

Those words spoken by my grandmother, however, continue to resonate with her today, and even though she still cries about her strict ways with her boys, the words of my late father still echo in her mind today as a constant reminder of the sincere gratitude he felt for all his mom and dad had done for him over the years.

As for parenting in the 21st century, Grandma doesn't think that kids are being guided as strictly as they should be. In fact, she will openly admit that "hardly any of them are," adding that strict parents are necessary to make the kids better.

That ruler above her kitchen door still hangs, but the dust that has collected on it over the last century gives testament to the fact that her two boys really were good kids. Grandma kept them so busy with activities that they scarcely had a moment to get into too much trouble!

"At the end of the day, they just wanted to go to bed," she laughed.

THE GREAT DEPRESSION

In recent years, our nation, as well as the world, has been in the midst of economic turmoil, and it bears painful remainders of the Great Depression of the 1930s for Grandma, but in a way far different than one might expect.

"Well, you know, we were lucky back then," she explained. "We had a drug store at that time. During those lean years that left so many people with little to nothing, Lloyd would not make his end of the week deposit at the bank. Instead, he would take any extra money he had and give it to others in town, you know...just a little bit to get by. We felt so lucky to be able to help so many people this way during those years. We didn't need to keep all of that money for ourselves."

The gift is in the giving. If you are able to share in your bounty with others, no matter how big or how small, you are the real recipient. Your reward comes in

the form of sheer delight in seeing other people happy. To this day, even when things are tight, I endeavor to share what I can with others. As Grandma has repeatedly told me, "You can't take it with you!" I honestly believe that if the world had more Kora and Lloyd Hollingers, things would be strikingly different.

REGRETS? WHO NEEDS 'EM?

Grandma has never harbored any regrets in life. The weight of that would only serve to slow her down anyway. She abided more by the philosophy that preached not to regret what you did do, but what you didn't do. She has always encouraged me to follow my heart, pursue my goals and dreams, and if I make a mistake or two along the way, or take a detour, learn from it and move on. Don't dwell on things like that.

Her spirited and upbeat attitude has always been the fuel of her soul.

"I always got whatever I wanted, as I knew I could" she said. "You just have to continue looking ahead in life. Make sure you always have something to do and somewhere to go, but don't forget to enjoy the moment."

Maybe it's a good thing that some folks tend to forget things in the past. They have probably just absorbed the lessons in those and have successfully moved on.

If Grandma had one simple recipe for living a long life, it would look something like this, in her words:

Eating

Not drinking

Always have a positive attitude

Always associate yourself with like-minded people

"You gotta get yourself with good people, the right people. That's just what you gotta do. Absolutely."

IN BETWEEN LOADS OF LAUNDRY AND A FOOTBALL GAME

It is amazing how much Grandma has always revealed about herself in her letters, even down to the smallest details, and she was never too shy about honestly expressing herself. This particular letter was sent to me in October of 1990, when I was relatively new to the Dallas area and was preparing for a new life down there, fresh out of graduate school and searching for a job. In the letter, she informs me of all that is going on with her and some of the extended family members.

October 21, 1990

Dear Ann:

Just finished doing a small load of laundry and before I go upstairs, wanted to write you a short letter.

Guess Judy and Blaine are in Japan by this time. They left yesterday for a week. I sure don't envy them going there. I have never been interested in Japan – the food!

I went to Salina Friday P.M. and stayed all night with Bob and Hazel. Took them out to Wyatt's to eat, and the next morn Bob and I went to Lawrence to the game. Said it was going to rain and be cold. So I took three coats and a rain coat. A winter one, an in-between one, and a light jacket, and three pairs of shoes, for rain or good, plus blankets, umbrellas, etc. We looked like we were going to stay a month.

It looked bad all the way to Lawrence, lightning and all, but all we got was a little sprinkle on us before the game and at the end of the third quarter when we were ready to leave.

I sat at the game with only my slacks and sweatshirt. Susan sat for quite a while with a short-sleeved blouse. It was a perfect day, except for the game, 41-10. KU played horribly. We played Colorado, but had a good picnic with Susan, L.A., and Steven. Justine wouldn't let Wash come. That seemed so strange for her. Came on to Salina and left Bob off and came on home in a drizzle all the way and was afraid it was going to get dark on me before getting home, and it was a little.

Another game this weekend and Bob may go with me again. I will see. I may then stay overnight Sat. and come home Sunday early morn, as we will gain an hour that morning, so could make it home in time for church to play the organ.

Sadie fell last Wednesday and was operated on that night for 3-4 hours for a blood clot on her brain. Is in intensive care, but I can't see how she would survive that kind of an operation. She will be 94 on Thanksgiving day, so put that down and send her a card, please. It doesn't have to be an expensive one, as she would not know the difference, but am sure Billy would appreciate you remembering her.

Had my club here last week and have the place decorated for Halloween stuff from when the kids were little. One night went to a dinner theater and saw "Steel Magnolias." It was great, as was the meal.

Did you watch the ball games and if so, did they suit you? They did for me, and I watched everyone to the end!

Well, enough. Please don't feel you have to answer every time I write. I'll still write to you, as I know you will be busy moving, getting your place fixed up and looking for work. All my love. Will now quit and RELAX a little. Going out for dinner tonight with two other couples.

Had a railing put on my back steps on the

east side of the house....for my friends...not for me. They all said they wouldn't come and see me if I didn't get one up. I may use it sometime later! I also had a light put right by the back door to leave on at night when I am out and can't see the key hole!

　　Grdma H

"THE PEST IS BACK!"

Ever since she married my dad, my mom has kept a guest book at her home for people to sign whenever they would stop by for a visit. Over the years, she has collected many of these books, and Grandma's signature can be seen numerous times in them, usually with some comment inscribed next to her name. Here's just a sampling of the guest book entries:

November 5, 1967 – Mother and Dad....Russell, KS (the pests!) Thanks to each and every one of you again. (En route home from Atlanta, GA)

November 13, 1970 – Grandparents Hollinger.....ate at McDonald's

November 26, 1970 – Grandparents Hollinger....not back again???

December 29, 1970 – Grandma and Grandpa Hollinger – "Memorable time!"

September 11, 1971 – Grandparents Hollinger – "Happy Birthday, Ann!"

December 17, 1980 – En route to Houston for Christmas

July 21, 1981 – En route to New York and Pennsylvania

September 11, 1981 – Here for Ann's birthday and Justine's birthday

October 9, 1981 - Not again!

February 3, 1982 – Headed for Palm Beach!

June 16, 1982 – Here we go again! Headed for Alabama and the World's Fair in Knoxville, TN

November 11, 1982 – En route to Houston while Blaine and Judy go to Athens

February 8, 1983 – Just me again, on my way to Palm Beach

May 2, 1983 – Went to Tulsa for Steve's graduation and then to Houston for Jeff's graduation

September 15, 1983 – Down for a football game!

January 4, 1984 – Headed for Houston

August 23, 1984 – En route to New York and Pennsylvania

September 6, 1984 – Made it back!

December 18, 1984 – On the road to Houston

December 29, 1984 – Back again!

March 22, 1985 – En route to Caribbean cruise

March 30, 1985 – Return from cruise

May 19, 1985 – Here for Ann's graduation!

May 29, 1985 – Off to New Hope, PA

August 27, 1985 - Headed for Canadian trip with Lil

November 24, 1985 – En route to Houston for turkey!

December 25, 1985 – Wonderful Christmas again

January 20, 1986 – En route home from Panama Canal Cruise! Fun!

December 15, 1986 – En route to Florida for Christmas!

December 28, 1986 – Back again!

March 1, 1987 – Home from Honolulu

April 20, 1987 – Where to now? San Francisco!

May 5, 1987 – Now ready for Houston

November 9, 1987 – Big day in Russell – Dole for President! Heading to Houston and then to L.A. to see Ann

February 1, 1988 – Not another trip!

March 3, 1988 – Home from Munich, Germany!

June 4, 1988 – Off on another Caribbean cruise!

July 7, 1988 – Is this all I do? Off to Pennsylvania

October 7, 1988 – Leaving for Cape Cod Tour

November 4, 1988 – Not again! Down for a KU-KSU game

November 19, 1988 – Headed for Houston for Thanksgiving! When I am dead and gone, will you remember all these visits?

April 30, 1989 – Off to Paris with Blaine!

May 14, 1989 – Home from Paris with Blaine!

June 15, 1989 – En route to New Orleans with Lillian

June 23, 1989 – Great trip on Miss. Queen N.O.

November 6, 1989 – Off for the trip of a lifetime. On Queen E2 to London! Spending my kids' inheritance; return home on Concorde

December 20, 1985 – Christmas in Houston and then in KC

July 31, 1990 – On my way to Greece

August 10, 1991 – Not here again!

December 27, 1991 – Return from Houston; purchased car; sad news of L.A.'s brain tumor

March 6, 1991 – En route to Florida with Ann

March 26, 1993 – Proud of L.A.! Down for L.A. Hollinger Day at Baptist Memorial Hospital

June 3, 1993 – Will miss you, L.A.; sad, but glad you didn't suffer

July 3, 1993 – In with bank tour group to Royals game and Dinner Theater

September 3, 1993 – Down for Ann's wedding – beautiful!

December 20, 1993 – Went with Susan to KU basketball game

December 27, 1993 - Missing you, L.A. Love you! (Are you getting tired of seeing my name in this guest book?)

May 12, 1994 – Down for dinner at Baptist for the first annual L.A. Hollinger, M.D. Scholarship Fund dinner. Bless you.

June 10, 1995 – Ready at 7:01 a.m. to start cruise with 14 of us!

February 15, 1996 – To Florida

February 22, 1997 – Headed to Palm Beach with Susan, Blaine, and Judy for my 92nd birthday

September 25, 1997 – Off to France with Blaine and Judy

December 12, 1997 – Going to Branson as Susan's guest

February 7, 1998 - Down to attend 100th anniversary celebration of KU Basketball; know you are getting tired of seeing my name in this book!

December 3, 1999 – Down to head off to Galveston to meet Billy and his new wife, Jane.

June 30, 2000 – Just ready to walk out the door with Susan and Steve for cruise

December 27, 2000 – Here for a KU basketball game

December 29, 2002 – Had a wonderful Christmas here with Susan, Steven, Ann, Ed, and boys

July 12, 2005 – Back from trip to Destin, FL with Blaine and Judy

October 6, 2005 – Back from Dorset, VT with Susan to see Billy and Jane's new home

June 12, 2008 – Here to speak at the L.A. Hollinger Scholarship annual dinner

December 5, 2009 – Here again for a visit

December 23, 2009 – Here for several days for Christmas (To date, this was her last visit to my mom's house. Grandma moved to Houston in 2010. As such, this is the last recorded entry, but you just never know with Grandma now, do you?)

At any rate, my mom assures me that Grandma was never a stranger. In the early days of her marriage to my dad, my mom noted that Grandma and Grandpa would frequently make the drive from Russell to Kansas City, practically every weekend, to spend time with them.

"No wonder it took me four years to get pregnant," sighed my mom.

Even on their wedding night, as my parents were settling into their hotel room for the night, they heard a loud knock at their door.

"Who could that be?" my mom inquired of my dad.

When my dad opened the door, he was surprised….yet, not really…to see his mom standing there, dressed up and ready to go.

"Are you ready to go out to eat?" she winked at him.

My dad just rolled his eyes and both and he and my mother got dressed and headed out with Grandma and Grandpa. (Evidently, Grandma had secured a room at the same hotel that night.)

My poor mom….she has graciously put up with a well-intentioned, yet sometimes meddling, mother-in-law through the years.

NOT ALWAYS THE WORDS I WANTED (OR NEEDED) TO HEAR

While Grandma has always been loving and kind to me, she was also quite strict with me, much like she was with my father in his younger days. However, I never doubted her genuine love for me. Yes, there were times when she upset me. She may have had an unpleasant word to say about something I was wearing or how I was behaving at a particular moment in time. She has always said what's on her mind, even if the words stung the person on the receiving end of them. That's just how she has been, and it is truly a part of her overall charm once you get to know her.

However, on June 7, 1993, a short dialogue I had with her will forever linger in my mind. It was actually more of a monologue than a dialogue, as she did most of the pontificating. I think the most I did was drop my jaw and make every effort to keep the tears from continually rolling down my face.

On that warm pre-summer's day, we buried my dad, L.A., just four days after he passed away from complications due to brain cancer. I had only seen Grandma this upset once before, and that was when Grandpa died in 1979. My dad was her rock, her anchor. She relied upon him for so much, and she was completely devastated when he told her in December 1991 that he had a very aggressive brain tumor that would most likely have a fatal outcome.

Over the course of the next 18 months, my dad lived out his life to the best of his abilities. Shortly before his diagnosis, he had sold his medical practice to assume an executive role within the hospital at which he worked. He was actually looking forward to spending more time with my mom and perhaps taking more vacations. After all, he was no longer on call at all hours of the day and night, and weekends suddenly became a welcome reality.

When we received the news that he was ill, we were all shocked. It seemed so unfair. How could a man so healthy, so active, and so vital have a brain tumor of this magnitude? While we all tried to remain optimistic, my dad's medical training and background clued him in as to the gravity of the situation. He knew in his heart that his time was limited, and in those final few weeks, it was so difficult to see him become but a whisper of the man he once was. He was 59 years old when he passed away, just 19 days shy of his 60th birthday.

On the day he died, I remember standing by his bedside in the hospital with my mom, my brother, my soon-to-be husband, Ed, and my grandmother, as well as a couple of nurses. As my dad took his final breath, I let out a scream and ran from the room. It was just too much to bear. My biggest fan was gone, taken away from me, and I was wondering how I would cope, even though I had months to prepare for this moment. I wanted more time.

The funeral was four days later on a Monday morning. After the ritual of burying him, we had a lunch at the church and then the immediate family retreated to my mom's home a few miles away to simply relax and absorb all that had happened in the last few days. It was very exhausting, as during this emotional time, I was working a full-time job and a part-time job, planning my September wedding, and building a new home with Ed.

As evening drew near, I gathered my things and headed out the door to my car so that I could go back to my apartment. Before I reached the front door, Grandma raced up to me and pulled me aside. The look on her face was something I had never really seen before. It was equal parts grief, anger, dismay, and disappointment.

She pointed a finger near my face and said, point-blank, "You did this. L.A. died because of you."

I was so shocked at this accusation that I was literally speechless.

She continued, "If you hadn't moved to Dallas and married that SOB, L.A. never would have gotten sick. The stress of everything you put him through caused him to get cancer. If you never put him through all of that, he would be alive today, of that I am most certain."

Then, she walked away. I realize in retrospect that she was merely talking through her extreme grief, but it hurt to have my grandmother speak to me like that. In all my years, she had never said such harsh words to me. She never has since that day, either.

I am strong enough to realize that her words were merely an outpouring of her heartache more than anything. Her son died and she needed something or someone to blame. I was an easy target, as my challenging life circumstances seemed to segue directly into my dad's diagnosis. I could see how she might make the connection.

I confided in my mom the next day as to what Grandma had said. She was obviously upset over it, too, but, like me, she reasoned that Grandma was so grief-stricken that those words were spoken before she could think rationally.

Grandma has never mentioned that incident since that day. I don't even think she would remember it now. I survived those words, however, and, if anything, what I have learned from them besides remembering it's very important to think before speaking, is to understand that we all deal with grief in strange ways. I also learned just how much she loved my dad from those words. Those words, heavy with hatred for my actions, were also heavy with love for my dad. If I could find a true sense of love in a conversation like that, then I knew I could continue to find the good in anything that should come my way in life. Grandma merely taught me, probably without realizing it at the time, that it's one's perspective that makes life good or bad. No one can ever take away your perspective. You simply have to know where to look.

"LET'S HIT THE SLOPES!"

Grandma's first (and last!) skiing adventure deserves appropriate elaboration. She never turns down an opportunity to add to her growing collection of life experiences. No matter what her age, if an adventure seemed exciting enough, she'd grab it! When the chance to go skiing for the first time came along in 1968, Grandma couldn't pack her bags quickly enough.

The story I have been told about this particular adventure is equal parts humorous and disappointing. Her first day on the slopes, Grandma quickly learned the ropes and was soon swooshing down the glistening snow, no doubt hooting and hollering all the way down with an unflappable grin that begged, "Look at me! Look at me!"

As she completed her final run for the day, she came to a quick stop at the base of the mountain, and in front of all the folks there, raised her arms above her head, ski poles in hand, and enthusiastically and triumphantly cheered herself on for such a grand exhibition of skill and athletic prowess.

As she jokingly thanked the crowds, she was unexpectedly hit from behind from a seemingly reckless skier who had evidently lost control, plowing right into Grandma. From triumph to tragedy, Grandma soon found herself flat on her back, crying and unable to move. She had broken her leg. That was the last time Grandma hit the slopes. Not that she was afraid to try it again. She enjoyed the experience, but it was merely something to cross off her bucket list. She was just proud to say she never actually fell while skiing.

"Just that dang uncontrollable fool behind me fell," she'd always remind us.

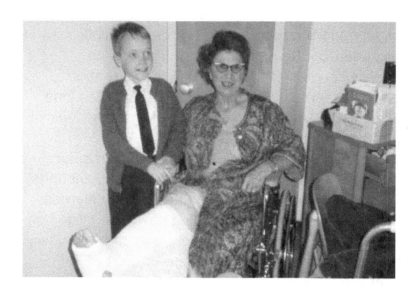

MY BROTHER STEVE, TENDING TO GRANDMA KORA AFTER SHE HAD SURGERY ON HER BROKEN LEG. GUESS THE NEXT WINTER OLYMPICS WOULD HAVE TO GO ON WITHOUT HER! NOTE THE BOX OF CARDS AND LETTERS BEHIND HER. GRANDMA HAS ALWAYS HAD A WAY ABOUT HER THAT COMPELS FOLKS TO SEND HER CARDS AND LETTERS FOR NEARLY EVERY SINGLE EVENT, OCCASION, AND MINOR CATASTROPHE IN HER LIFE. SHE HAS ALWAYS ENJOYED BRAGGING ABOUT HOW MANY CARDS AND LETTERS SHE GETS IN THE MAIL FOR BIRTHDAYS, HOLIDAYS, ETC. YOU'D THINK SHE WAS A CELEBRITY OR SOMETHING!

MY PERSONAL "KORASPONDENCE" TO MYSELF

Ann Butenas' Journal Entry: Thursday, December 4, 2008:

What a serendipitous world in which we live! The Universe works in mysterious ways. Let me tell you about my day today.

First of all, I was to have attended a meeting with an individual with whom I am doing some writing work. I have been working on this project for several weeks now, and was geared up to move forward to the final piece at this particular appointment this morning. However, a few weeks ago, I was asked to join a local Chamber of Commerce. I was reluctant to do so earlier this year, as I did not want to spend the money. Well, they had a special offer now, so I signed up. I subsequently got some materials in the mail, but did not look them over thoroughly for several days.

It finally dawned on me that perhaps I should look all of that over, so two days ago, I read the information that was sent to me and realized that all new members of late would be introduced at their next event, which was today.

Realizing I already had a commitment at that time, I simply told myself that I would just skip the Chamber event. Nonetheless, something continued to nag me that perhaps I SHOULD attend the event. Then, when I realized if I went to the event, as a new member, I could stand before the large crowd and talk about what I do. Well, I could not miss that opportunity, so I asked the guy with whom I was doing the writing project if I could bow out of this week's particular meeting. He had no problem with that.

So, this morning, I headed on over to the Chamber event, which was held at a local retail store. The crowd was large! I grabbed a muffin and began to mingle. Soon, the director made some announcements and then invited all of the new members to come up and give their infomercials. There were about ten of us who did that, and I was the last one to present. I really enjoyed being up there in front of everyone with the microphone in hand! Love a good crowd!

After the presentations, everyone at the event returned to mingling and networking. A gal soon came up to me and handed me a piece of paper announcing a special Christmas sale for her business. Being polite, yet privately not interested, I took the sheet of paper. I wanted to throw it away when she was out of sight, but instead, I folded it up and stashed it in my purse, thinking I would toss it out when I got home.

After more socializing, I headed out to the car, intending to go home. Half-way home, I realized that I had to mail something to someone in town. I looked at the address I had written on the envelope and noticed that her house was actually on my way home, so I just decided to drop it off at her home.

After leaving her home, I made my way towards my house. I thought about going to Target on the way back home to get some Christmas shopping done. I then told myself that, no, I had to get home to get some work done. However, I was soon near the Target store en route home and something just made me turn into the parking lot. "I guess I have to go in now," I mused to myself.

I parked the car and hurried across the parking lot in the brisk cold air. As I was walking into the store, I realized my cell phone was on vibrate mode, so I turned it back on to the ring tone mode and threw it back in my purse. Lucky move....as if it was on vibrate, I never would have known it went off, buried deep in my purse. With the ring tone on, at least I could hear it when someone called me.

I made my way through the store and began to pick out a few items. I soon heard my phone ringing. I rummaged through my purse, picked up the phone, and saw the caller ID message as "District of Columbia." I knew right then who it was. "Oh, dear...here I am in Target in the dog food aisle, and 'You Know Who' is calling me!"

I calmly (yeah, right!) answered my phone. It was "You Know Who's" assistant, telling me that "You Know Who" wanted to chat with me. In a brief instant, I was panic-stricken, but as she put me through to former US Republican Presidential candidate and US Senator and Majority Leader, Bob Dole, a wave of composed professionalism swept over me.

Thank goodness Senator Dole could not see me fumbling through my purse, looking for a pen. "I know there is one in here. There HAS to be one in here," I thought to myself. I finally found one and then thought, "Oh, no! What do I write on now?" Remember, Senator Dole has just said "hello," and I have responded accordingly, as calmly as possible, yet I am frantically in the dog food aisle, looking for a pen and hoping no one would announce a price check or store special over the intercom. God forbid the Senator actually knew where I was. After all, I AM a professional!

Next on my frantic agenda, as I continued to stall the conversation with "How are you" and "What is the weather like there," I looked for something upon which to write. Then, I found it! That darn piece of paper that gal at the Chamber gave to me that I had originally wanted to throw away! "Thank goodness for a poinsettia sale today!" I laughed to myself when looking at the printed side of the paper.

I hurriedly found a small space on a shelf in the dog food aisle between the Milk Bones and the chew toys on which to write. I turned the piece of paper over and readied my pen. Now, I could interview this national figure head.

For the most part, it was a very informal conversation. We chatted about many things, from my grandma, to his life in Russell, to chatty politicians in Washington, D.C. Yes, even President-elect Obama's name came up in conversation. It was an experience I shall never forget.

Among the things he shared with me about my grandparents both surprised me and inspired me. He referred to Grandma as always on "full throttle."

"My recollection of her back in the day is somewhat akin to the Energizer Bunny," he laughed.

I reminded him that she had yet to slow down.

Senator Dole continued, "Kora did everything in town. Everyone knew her. From all accounts, she was a great mom to L.A. and Blaine and a great wife to Sal." (I'll tell you all about "Sal" soon!)

What touched me more than anything was his unique relationship with Grandpa. I know my grandfather touched so many people during his life, but I never really understood the depth of his presence until Senator Dole conveyed to me just how special Grandpa really was.

"Your grandfather may never have known it, but I had a special relationship with him for years," explained Senator Dole. "As a young boy, I specifically picked him out as the guy in town who I wanted to be around. I really respected him. I simply enjoyed hanging around him and just talking with him for hours. He was a very quiet man, but strong in presence."

As for his relationship with my grandmother, the Senator noted that Grandma was not one to sympathize easily with others.

I reminded him she is still that way.

"That's not to say Kora was never nice or kind, as she most definitely was," he noted. "She just never stood for much pity."

I reminded him that she still doesn't allow for pity.

He indicated that Grandma was definitely a hard worker and managed the Hollinger Drug Store like a President runs a country.

One of his most prominent memories about Grandma was back during World War II.

"When I returned home from the war," he said, "I was bed-ridden for a while, and Kora came by the house to see me. Everyone else would express their concerns and sympathy for me, but not Kora. No...she just looked at me and told me to get off my rear end...that I had things to do and that I better get to them. She would never in a million years say something like 'you poor thing.' She was polite, but she would never say anything like that. Just wasn't her style."

More than anything, Senator Dole will always recall my grandmother as a very positive person.

"She always gave people hope and inspiration," he said.

I reminded him that she still does.

"She is also a great inspiration to the senior citizens of our country," he emphasized.

He then recounted a meeting he recently had in West Virginia with a 107-year-old World War I survivor, the sole survivor of that war, actually.

"I listened to that gentleman give a speech," the Senator said. "Unlike your grandmother, he was a man of very few words." He then paused momentarily and laughed, "We could use him in the Senate, you know!"

Towards the end of our dialogue, I asked Senator Dole, if Grandma ever decided to run for office, how did he think her speech would go?

"If Kora ever gave a speech, it would probably be something like this: 'Hello. Good-bye. Now get the hell out of here!'" he joked.

Both of us decided that perhaps we should arrange an introduction between Grandma and that World War I veteran, but then I remembered that Grandma was considering moving soon and would be quite busy for a while. That really got Senator Dole on a roll...

"How many folks her age say that they want to move out of state and start over?" he kidded.

I reminded him that Grandma just got her second wind!

Ford Picks Bob Dole

The Russell Daily News

Kansas Delegation Elated

Carlson Surprised But Happy

Soviets Contend Voting Is Rejection

COURTESY RUSSELL DAILY NEWS... AUG 19, 1976

The Russell Daily News

County Has New Producer

Mayor Williams Arrives In Time

Russell to Host Elks Meeting

Mrs. Dole Ponders

Member of Ford's Staff Has Different Idea About Russell

COURTESY RUSSELL DAILY NEWS... AUG 21, 1976

COURTESY RUSSELL DAILY NEWS... AUG 23, 1976

COURTESY RUSSELL DAILY NEWS... SEP 19, 1991 GRANDMA
KORA, SEATED FAR RIGHT, HAVING COFFEE WITH KANSAS
SENATOR ROBERT J. DOLE. OF COURSE, IT'S AT THE TABLE
AND REFRESHMENTS APPEAR TO BE INVOLVED!

WHO WAS SAL? (FURTHER INSIGHT FROM BOB DOLE!)

As I was working on this book, I had the honor of speaking with a very special individual known across the country and around the world, former US Senate Majority Leader and US Presidential candidate, Bob Dole.

During our 30-minute phone conversation in the fall of 2008, I noticed that he frequently referred to my late grandfather as "Sal." Growing up, that was all anyone ever called my grandfather, whose real name was Lloyd. Wherever we went, it was always "Hi, Sal!" or "Nice to see you, Sal." I always wondered why they called him by that name, and frequently inquired of others as to why, but no one seemed to really know the reason behind the moniker.

Getting bolder in my discussion with Senator Dole, I asked him, "I noticed that you frequently have referred to my grandfather as 'Sal.' Why is that?"

Senator Dole politely responded, "Well, that is what everyone always called him. It is actually short for 'Sally.'"

By now I was wondering if there was something unusual about my grandfather that folks kept hidden from me. My long pause in the dialogue gave Senator Dole an opportunity to continue the topic.

"Do you know what a 'Sally' is?" he asked of me.

Yet another long pause on my end. Sensing my ignorance, Senator Dole happily filled in the blanks for me.

"A 'Sally' is someone who is always doing something for others. If someone needs a helping hand, that 'Sally' is there. It is someone who is giving of service to others. That was your grandfather. That was 'Sal.'"

"I know for a fact that if someone called your grandfather in the middle of the night to have a prescription filled, he would fill it," said Senator Dole. "If a customer could not come by the pharmacy to pick up a prescription, your grandfather would personally deliver it to them."

This undying attitude of service enabled my grandfather to run a very successful pharmacy for over 40 years, even thriving during the Great Depression. Sure, there was a bigger and fancier pharmacy just 20 minutes away, but folks still came back to my grandfather's store, time and time again. Maybe it was the service. Maybe it was Grandpa's dog, Snoopy, who happily greeted each customer who walked into the store. Maybe it was to simply sit and chat with "Sal" for a few minutes while he filled a prescription.

Senator Dole then elaborated about how my grandfather's attitude of service extended into how he conducted his career over the next several decades. Now, if you think about it, that attitude of service and commitment to others, to his constituents (his customers!), led him to running against former US President Bill Clinton for the most powerful position in the world.

What can an attitude of "Sally" do for you throughout your life? My name is Sally. What's yours?

SO MANY LIVES TOUCHED THROUGHOUT THE YEARS

In early 2010, I received a wonderful letter from a lady who used to live in Russell near my grandmother when she was a child. The insight she provides in this letter accurately conveys the character of my grandmother and late grandfather.

Maryville, Illinois

February 13, 2010

Our father was an oil field pumper, and our family of six lived in a small lease house west of Russell in what was then the country. Now, as an adult, I fully appreciate and admire Kora and Sal for their generosity. I probably would never have seen the inside of the Tower Care had it not been for them including us from time to time for lunch after church on Sunday. Also, Sal hired me to work at the drug store for two summers so I could earn money for my tuition to attend our church college in York, Nebraska. We were never treated differently because of our lack of resources.

In 2000, my late husband, Tom, and I were in Russell for the 50th reunion of my high school class of 1950. We attended the worship service on Sunday at the Methodist Church. It happened to

be the first Sunday when Kora was no longer the
organist, so we sat with her. She didn't know
what to do with the attendance pad because it
was new to her!

She invited us to go out to eat with her for
lunch. When we arrived at the restaurant, she
suggested (no, TOLD) us to take the buffet because
of the fried chicken, but she ordered from the
menu! We had a good time and lots of laughter.

Tom, who several years earlier, had suffered a
major heart attack, dutifully removed the skin
from his chicken and placed it near the edge of
his plate. Kora sized up the situation and asked,
"Aren't you going to eat that skin?" Tom told her
it was bad for him. Kora promptly reached over
to transfer it to her own plate and Tom
cautioned, "Not good for you, either," to which
Kora responded, "My dear boy, I've been eating
fried chicken skin all my life and it hasn't
bothered me yet!"

She proceeded to eat it all!

What a funny, interesting, curious,
adventurous, sports-loving, dedicated church
worker and role model she has been for many of

us who grew up in the United Brethren Church, now the United Methodist Church, in Russell, Kansas.

I am so grateful for the afternoon visits and annual Christmas letter exchange we have had since I left Russell permanently in 1952.

Sincerely,

Jean M.S.

THAT'S MY BOY!!!

Never before has there existed a bigger cheerleader of her children than Kora Hollinger. Throughout her two boys' academic careers, whenever they were involved in sports of any kind, Grandma was in the stands, cheering them on! Some town folks eventually learned to not sit too close to her in the stands, as she would invariably at several points during a basketball or football game jab the person next to her in the ribs with her elbow and proudly proclaim, "That's my boy!" as a winning play was made.

Grandma continued her enthusiastic cheerleading efforts as her boys participated in sports on the collegiate level, too. Uncle Blaine was a star track athlete and basketball player while a student at the University of Kansas. He played basketball there when Wilt Chamberlin did. Grandma and Grandpa always made sure to make the drive from Russell to Allen Field House in Lawrence, Kansas, to cheer on the home team!

Grandma also attended most every single home football game at the University of Kansas for decades. Neither of her boys played on the college football team, but she has always been a die-hard Jayhawks fan, through and through. I remember I wore a purple dress once to an event she was hosting back when I was a teenager, and she demanded that I change clothes, as purple was the color associated with Kansas State University, and she did not want to be associated with that! She takes those KU Jayhawks very seriously and is so proud of them.

When I was growing up, I frequently went to KU football games with my family. We had several season tickets, so in addition to my parents, myself, and Grandma and Grandpa Hollinger, my maternal grandparents, Wash and Justine Brown, were also on hand, as they were also season ticket-holders for both football and basketball games. Yes....it was truly a family affair....for many, many years.

Saturday afternoons in the fall were quite the ritual in our family. On game day, Grandma and Grandpa would awaken early and commence the nearly four hour drive from Russell to Lawrence, meeting us just in time in the stadium parking lot so we could all tailgate and have a good meal before the game. It was such an interesting dynamic to see the variety of personalities between both sets of grandparents. On the one hand, we had loud and exuberant Kora and on the other hand, we had sweet, quiet, and petite Justine, my mom's mom. Never before was there such an odd, yet seemingly compatible pairing. While in the stadium, Grandma Justine would sit properly and quietly, never drawing attention to herself. She was always dressed well and never seemed to have a hair out of place. Seated next to her would by my grandpa Brown. Tall, slender, and a man of genuine character, he would sit next to his "bride," dressed impeccably for the occasion - sport coat, bow tie, and hat. He was rarely seen in those days without his pipe, either. That was his trademark. I found it interesting how my dad, a pulmonary physician, was able to tolerate that, but he graciously did. For some reason, the smoking habit was the last thing you really noticed about Grandpa Brown anyway.

In the seats in front of Grandpa and Grandma Brown would be Grandma and Grandpa Hollinger. This is where the fun begins. Grandma Kora was never shy about voicing her opinion about the players, the coaches, the overall game, and even the cheerleaders. Most of the time, she'd be on her feet, yelling, screaming, and carrying on. Yes, my mom did tell me it was embarrassing on occasion and that at one point during a game, a stranger next to her asked her, "Is that your mother?" My mom politely responded, "No, this one is," as she turned around and gestured towards Justine. The stranger, realizing my mom was equally subdued, nodded, "I should have known."

Yes...I do believe that during those fall college football games up at the University of Kansas, Grandma Kora was the one who got everyone to do the wave....the wheat wave. If you've never seen this, it's like a flash mob in the open prairie. Everyone in the stadium will stand and raise their arms above their heads and wave them back and forth as if to resemble wheat stalks blowing in the wind. If you ever do experience this type of celebration, make sure you have used deodorant that day...and wear ear plugs if you find yourself seated next to Grandma.

LATE 1950S....THE THREE BEAUTY QUEENS
LEFT TO RIGHT: JUSTINE BROWN, SUSAN HOLLINGER, KORA
HOLLINGER

GRANDPA AND GRANDMA BROWN BACK IN THE DAY!

EVEN AT 102 YEARS OF AGE, GRANDMA MADE SURE TO SEND OUT HER ANNUAL CHRISTMAS LETTER

December 2007

Merry Christmas to all!

Well, I'm still here. I can't see or hear, but I am living at home and I am in very good health. I have my lady come in and help for two hours Monday through Friday, but I still do all my own cooking and of course my appetite is still very good. I attend Sunday school and church every Sunday and I still go to Circle once a month. I am still going with friends to McDonald's for Saturday morning coffee and also on Wednesday night.

Our Bridge-O-Rama started in September. We have 12 couples that play. I have hosted it three times this year. I still try to attend a KU basketball game when I can get Catherine Holland to take me or bring me home from trips. I still don't miss a KU game on TV!

I have been busy going places all year. In May, I went to Dallas to Cindy's wedding. Blaine and Judy were also there. I stayed with them for three weeks. After the wedding, Blaine, Judy, and I flew to Wichita for the Hollinger reunion. The reunion was at Bob and Karen Henderson's. It is northeast of Wichita, in the Blue Hills. They have a beautiful home with cabins. We stayed in the cabins. They were very nice, with air conditioning, bathrooms, and everything we needed. There were 50 people at the reunion. Dean Hollinger, Marylyn Swartz, Patty, and his niece drove me home from the reunion before they returned to their home in Colorado.

In July, we had our yearly week vacation in Estes Park, Colorado. Blaine has supported this yearly vacation for the past 20 years. We had a wonderful time, as usual.

In August, I had the honor bestowed upon me to be the House Mother for Blaine's Phi Delta Theta pledge reunion. I met Blaine and Judy in Denver. It was a four-day affair and was held at a beautiful resort area.

In November, I flew to Houston to be with Blaine and Judy for Thanksgiving. All 15 members of the family were there.

I have had a lot of Christmas socials already this December, including parties at both banks, Edward D. Jones, the Elks Club, and the church. I am planning on going to Susan's house for Christmas.

I am still going strong for someone who will be 103 years old on February 22, 2008. I wish you all a very blessed Christmas and a Happy New Year.

Love,

Kora

PUTTING IT INTO PERSPECTIVE!

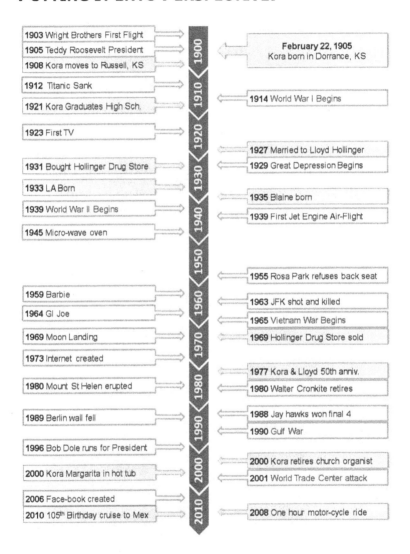

1903 Wright Brothers First Flight	1900	February 22, 1905 Kora born in Dorrance, KS
1905 Teddy Roosevelt President		
1908 Kora moves to Russell, KS		
1912 Titanic Sank	1910	1914 World War I Begins
1921 Kora Graduates High Sch.		
1923 First TV	1920	
		1927 Married to Lloyd Hollinger
1931 Bought Hollinger Drug Store	1930	1929 Great Depression Begins
1933 LA Born		
		1935 Blaine born
1939 World War II Begins	1940	1939 First Jet Engine Air-Flight
1945 Micro-wave oven		
	1950	1955 Rosa Park refuses back seat
1959 Barbie	1960	1963 JFK shot and killed
1964 GI Joe		1965 Vietnam War Begins
1969 Moon Landing		1969 Hollinger Drug Store sold
1973 Internet created	1970	
		1977 Kora & Lloyd 50th anniv.
1980 Mount St Helen erupted	1980	1980 Walter Cronkite retires
1989 Berlin wall fell	1990	1988 Jay hawks won final 4
		1990 Gulf War
1996 Bob Dole runs for President		2000 Kora retires church organist
2000 Kora Margarita in hot tub	2000	2001 World Trade Center attack
2006 Face-book created	2010	2008 One hour motor-cycle ride
2010 105th Birthday cruise to Mex		

"EVER HEAR OF THE WORD 'POTATO?'"

When I called Grandma to wish her a HAPPY 106th BIRTHDAY in February 2011, her sense of humor was still going strong! She cracks me up! She loves to talk about her favorite subject - food! When I asked her if she was getting good meals where she now lives, she said, "I had to ask the cook just the other day, 'Have you ever heard of the word potato?'" She LOVES her potatoes, and she was getting tired of the macaroni stuff on the menu. She wants her potatoes! And steak! And chip chocolate pie! Nothing like "good eatin'!" (And Grandma will frequently remind us that the day she loses interest in eating is the day we should begin to worry!)

GRANDMA, ENJOYING THE POTATO AT A HOUSTON FAST FOOD JOINT, 2010.

GRANDMA HAS THE SECRET FOR LOOKING YOUNGER IN PHOTOS!

No matter what your age, I am sure that many of you have seen photos of yourself and thought, "Wow! I look older than I realized!" Admit it! It happens. For me, at age 47, it happens more than I would like to think. However, I recently discovered from Grandma how to look positively radiant in a photo, without overly-done makeup or photo shop techniques.

A few years ago, when Grandma was a mere pup of 103 years, it was time for her to have her picture taken for the church directory in her home town. Not one known for her shyness, Grandma was up to the task. After all, she loves photo opportunities and has trained me to make sure I have a photo of her at some prominent spot in my home. (However, I feel that the photo I do have on the wall is just her way of "watching me" and making sure I am behaving! She always assumes mischief is on my radar, when it is actually on hers!)

So, in an effort to look positively charming for the big photo, Grandma spent some time in her bathroom, tending to her thinning blue hair and putting on her blush (and I swear it is the same product from the 1970s) and some green lipstick. What? Green lipstick? Oh, she is proud of that little item. She bought it several years ago off of some TV ad. The actual lipstick is green, but it turns to a complementary shade of red once applied to the lips. She simply bought it for its inherent shock value. "I love to put this on while in public to see what kinds of reaction I will get when folks see me applying green lipstick to my lips," she grinned.

Once she approved of her final look, she had a friend drive her to the photo shoot location. The photographer ushered her in and had her sit on a somewhat comfortable stool, positioning her "just so" and adjusting the lighting. After a few shots were taken, Grandma was satisfied that she did well and was resting her hopes of looking even more glamorous in the hands of the photographer. Being the oldest person to be featured in the church directory was the equivalent to her of winning the Noble Prize or something.

A few days later, Grandma was treated to the proofs of her photos. "By golly, if my photo is going to be in the church directory that will probably still be circulating when I am six feet under, I want to leave a good looking legacy," she commented.

To her dismay, the photos horrified her. "My god!" she proclaimed. "I look so dang old!"

The photographer explained to Grandma that through the use of digital technology and certain computer tricks, he could easily minimize the look of her obvious fine lines and wrinkles.

Without missing a beat, my financially savvy grandma asked, "How much is that gonna cost me?"

When the photographer told her "about $100.00," Grandma took matters into her own hands.

She grabbed the stool upon which she had sat a few days earlier and moved it just a few feet further away from the camera and sat down, put on a big smile (and more green lipstick!) and demanded of the photographer, "Now take my picture!"

Amazing! Just moving a few feet back from the prying eye of the camera, Grandma's lines and wrinkles were hardly noticeable! She was pleased, and the church directory would live in glorious distinction! Thank God! (No, literally! Thank God! After all, it IS a church directory!)

ON TRAVELING

"I love to travel. Everyone should get out there and see the world. We made it a point to take L.A. and Blaine to as many places as possible, even Cuba! Don't ask me why we took them there; we just did.

The problem with traveling these days, however, rests in the historical sites I might explore. It's no fun looking at things that are younger than I am!"

GRANDPA AND GRANDMA, SAILING ON THE ATLANTIC, CIRCA 1970.

THE ONE THING TO ALWAYS REMEMBER – THE ULTIMATE ANTI-AGING SECRET

"Keep on working in your life. Keep on living. Have something to do. Otherwise, you'll just go downhill from there. You can stay young in all that you do, think, and say. You can stay forever young in your mind. Just because you get older doesn't mean you have to BE older!"

GEE, GRANDMA...IS THE REAL SECRET TO A HEALTHY LONG LIFE EVIDENCED BY THE BAG OF DOG FOOD BEHIND YOU? IS THAT "GOOD EATIN'?"

GRANDMA SPEAKS HER MIND AND MAKES THE NEWS!

August 1988 – From the Russell Daily News

Fossil Street Resident Recalls Earlier Paving

Mrs. Kora Hollinger, life-long Fossil Street resident, says she is the only one now still living along the street who has seen it paved twice. The first time was around 1925. Crews applied paving brick, cushioned by a layer of sand atop a layer of concrete. This time, the street is being widened and paved with additional storm were drainage provided.

The street project resulting in major changes in routing of major electrical, water, gas and sewer lines.

"My intersection will be the first to be opened. They say the Second Street crossing will be opened to traffic Monday and I plan to be there at 7 a.m. to be the first one to drive across it," Mrs. Hollinger said.

"I'll bet the paving they are doing this time won't last 64 years like the brick did," Mrs. Hollinger added.

THESE WERE THE GUIDELINES BY WHICH KORA WAS ADVISED, PRESUMABLY GIVEN TO HER BY A PEDIATRICIAN, TO TAKE CARE OF HER BOYS WHEN THEY WERE TODDLERS. NOTICE THIS DOCUMENT WAS "REVISED" IN 1930.

Chart No. 14 (Revised February, 1930)

HANG THIS WHERE YOU CAN SEE IT EVERY DAY

1 Year to 18 Months

CHILD'S DAILY TIME CARD

7.00 a. m. . . . . Toilet. Wash and dress. Brush teeth.

7.30 a. m. . . . . BREAKFAST: Cooked cereal with milk and little or no sugar; toast; coddled or soft-boiled egg; crisp bacon occasionally; boiled whole milk.
Plain cod-liver oil, then orange juice or tomato juice (before or after breakfast).
Toilet. Play.

9.00 a. m. . . . . Bath. (Bath may be given at 7 a. m. if more convenient.)

9.30 a. m. . . . . Out of doors until dinner. Sun bath during morning.

10.45 a. m. . . . . Boiled whole milk. (If dinner is at 12, this milk should be given at 3.30 p. m. (See note below.)

11.00 a. m. . . . . Toilet. Nap for 2 hours, in sun if weather permits. (If dinner is at 12, the nap should be at 12.30.) Toilet.

1.00 p. m. . . . . DINNER: Green vegetable, baked potato, rice, or plain boiled macaroni; meat or fish (three times a week); simple pudding; boiled whole milk.

1.30 p. m. . . . . Toilet. Out of doors as long as weather permits, in sun except on very hot days. Play.

5.00 p. m. . . . . Toilet. Undress for night. Wash.

5.30 p. m. . . . . SUPPER: Cooked cereal or rice; milk-vegetable soup or boiled whole milk; toast; raw or cooked fruit.
Plain cod-liver oil, then orange juice or tomato juice (before or after supper).
Brush teeth.

6.00 p. m. . . . . Toilet. Bed, lights out, windows open, door shut.

This plan may be varied to suit the family schedule, but one like this should be arranged and kept to closely. Some little children may do better to have milk and toast at 6 a. m., breakfast at 9, dinner at 1, and supper at 5. Whatever plan is used, meals should be at the same time every day.

U. S. DEPARTMENT OF LABOR
CHILDREN'S BUREAU
C. B. 120
(See other side)

ON THE RECEIVING END

Even though Grandma has always fancied herself the consummate letter-writer, she has been on the receiving end of such things many times throughout the years. However, if you intend to write her a letter or send her a card, it better be worth reading. She does not stand for greeting cards sent through the mail that only have just a signature and nothing else. In fact, in the past, she has been known to "return to sender" a card that did not have at least a brief note or some written correspondence in it.

Her basic rules of sending her mail consisted of the following:

*Write at least one page telling her all that you have done.

*Be sure to write down anything interesting you have eaten since the last communication.

*Tell her you'll write again soon.

*Don't just sign your name. Draw a little smiley face or cartoon. (This rule was for me only. I began this habit as a child, and to this day, whenever I send her a letter, I make sure to draw a smiley face at the end of it.)

My signature sign-off in letters was always "Love, Ann" followed by a smiley-face ☺. A couple of times, just to test her, instead of writing a note in a birthday card I sent to her, I drew a note...a musical note, and when she would later call me to jokingly reprimand me for not including any "news" in my letter, I'd say, "Well, you told me to include a note, so I draw a quarter note. I even threw in a whole note. What's the problem?"

One short letter I sent to her was immediately withdrawn from the "to-be-mailed" pack of letters by my mom when I was seven years old. Here's how it read:

September 11, 1970

Dear Grandma and Grandpa:

Thank you for the new piggy bank for my birthday. I now have seven of them.

Love,

Ann ☺

What? I wrote a note, thanked them for the gift, and drew a smiley face. Acceptable, right? Guess I wasn't supposed to let Grandma and Grandpa know that they gave me something that I already had in vast multiples!

Even Grandpa sent Grandma a few love letters back in the roaring twenties when they were temporarily separated by the demands of his budding career. Here's one I came across:

July 28, 1927

Ponca City, OK

My Dearest Kora:

Just finished reading your letter of the 26th and incidentally I had a very fine lunch so you see I should feel in a mood to write you. If you officiate my letters as much as I do yours, I know how you would feel if you didn't get one every day. When I left you, I didn't think I'd write you one each day but so far I haven't had much difficulty. Guess it just comes naturally to me to want to get a letter written to my girl each day.

Sorry to hear that you still have such an awful cold. You better go see Dr. C. about it and get some medicine so you can get some relief from it. You will feel better and be able to stand the long drive back.

Honey, I know you are enjoying yourself immensely at home but I would much rather you would be here cause it is just too darn lonesome down here for me. All I can do is read or go to a show you know. This isn't living. I probably kid you a lot about wanting to be a bachelor, etc., but I can tell the world I would rather have you dear than anything else in the world, and I don't mean perhaps.

I went to the Murray last night. Enjoyed the show very much. Wish you could have been with me for I know you, too, would have enjoyed it. They had a kinda style show...with a display of fur coats showing them on models. Think they had about 25 coats and were supposed to be about $20,000 worth of furs. Got home about 11.

So you say nothing has happened to you and it is the 26th. Don't worry, cause everything will be OK. You have just had a little too much excitement.

Things must be getting bad between Mr. and Mrs. T. The way things are, guess it is just as well that they do live apart and get a divorce.

Well, honey, have reached my limit so will sign off. Guess maybe I will write you tomorrow.

Yours,

Lloyd

A REFLECTION OF 100 YEARS IN ONE AFTERNOON

How did Grandpa ask you to marry him?

(Laughs) He didn't! I asked him! Actually we talked about it together and when he got his first pharmacy job in Oklahoma, we decided to get married. The timing was perfect.

Where did you get married?

In my mom's house. It was a small gathering.

Was there ever anything in life that you really desired but never obtained?

I never wanted for much. I have had a good life, a great life. It seemed that whatever I wanted was always there for me.

Was there ever something you received in life that you did not want?

You bet! One year I was really hoping to get a fancy new bridge table, and I got dishes or something practical instead!

Have you ever been afraid of anything in your life?

Nope! Can't think of a thing!

What has been the most difficult challenge you have had in life?

You know, I have had just a normal life. Honest to God, a normal life. People tell me the darndest tales, and I don't have a thing like that to tell people.

What is the best thing you have done in your life?

Marrying Lloyd. We had such a lovely life, lovely children, you know.

What type of career did you have when you were younger?

I had my own business. I was a courthouse stenographer. I loved having my own business. I had some really good times back in the oil boom days. We had a door in our drug store that led directly into the hotel next door, and when folks would come to town and needed secretarial or stenographic work done, I'd head over there and get that done. Busy life! (She made $75.00 a month back in the 1920s! She also would occasionally take the train to Salina, Kansas and teach piano lessons to kids for 50 cents a lesson.)

If you could say anything to your son, L.A., who passed away in 1993, what would you say to him?

I miss you, honey. I really miss you. I hope I see you soon.

Did you ever image that you would live this long?

Never dreamed I'd even make it to 90. Back in those days, people didn't live this long. I can't figure it out, honesty.

What is your favorite meal?

There isn't one thing I can say that is not my favorite! I love anything and everything. However, I will not eat raw oysters or sushi.

What is your favorite time of the year?

I suppose Spring. Everything is green, warm, and beautiful.

If you could meet anyone in the world whom you've never met, who would it be?

Oh, I'm not particular. I like meeting everyone.

Who is the most famous person you've met?

Well, I've met lots of important people... presidents, celebrities.....difficult to answer this one.

What is your favorite sport to watch?

(Grins) Basketball! Football, too!

What is your favorite sport to play?

(Smiles) All of them! I was a great basketball player in high school. Our team took second in the state, you know.

When you look back over your life, is there any one particular time or period that stands out above the rest that brings back fond memories?

You know, my life has been a very good life, a smooth life. Nobody has lived such a life as I have.

Do you remember going to the movies when you were younger?

You mean the talkies? Oh, sure. When Lloyd and I lived in Oklahoma, I worked for the Ford Motor Company, and one evening my boss let us take a brand new Lincoln out on the town. We went to see "The Jazz Singer," I believe it was. We had a great time!

What's been your favorite car over the years?

My Cadillacs! I love Cadillacs! I've enjoyed driving every single one of them that I've had. I have one in the garage right now. (Her first car was a brand new 1927 four-door Chevrolet that she purchased for $400.00)

Do you have a best friend?

I have had many good friends in my life, but they all have passed on now. I'd say that Bobbi Beardsley was probably my best pal, but she died young, too.

What do you think Heaven is like?

Topsy-turvy. However, I think when answering that question we are supposed to say that it is wonderful and that it is better than any place to which we have ever been.

What do you think about most now?

Dying. At my age, you have plenty of time to think about that.

How do you envision your funeral to be?

Beautiful.

What do you think people will say about you when you are gone?

That I was terrible! I just hope they have good things to say about me. I've been a good person, I believe.

What do you most admire about yourself?

I'm pretty darn honest. Definitely honest. I pay people back, and I have stressed being honest over the years to my kids. My parents did that with me, and I did that with my boys.

What do you like least about yourself?

(Laughs) That I'm so darn homely! Yes, I am. Outside of that, the one thing I really regret in life is that I didn't pursue the Olympics. I feel that I really could've done something in that regard. Even when I hear what athletes are doing these days, I know I could have accomplished the same thing. Don't know why I never pursued it and wish I had.

Is there anything you were ever afraid to try?

No. I could do anything that I set my mind to do. I always knew I was pretty smart. I started college at 16. I went to Washburn in Topeka. Didn't finish, though, but a few years later, a friend of mine convinced me to enroll in a business school in Salina, which I did. I do pretty well for myself, you know!

In fact, when I was 103 years of age, my grandson asked me if I wanted to go for a ride on his motorcycle. He wanted to help me get up on it, saying I needed the help. I said, "Wanna bet? Watch me." And I got up on it. I made it all on my own. I knew I could do it. That's the way I have been my whole life. If you believe in yourself, how can you fail? Not possible.

Do you believe that you can get whatever you want out of life?

I do believe that. Believe.

If you could relive one era in your life, what period of time would that be?

When my kids were smaller. I really enjoyed doing family things, going places, and being together. That's what it's all about.

Of what are you most afraid in life?

Can you give me a few examples of things that should scare me? I honestly don't know. I have no fears of anything. Nothing bothers me. I'm just lucky that way.

What piece of advice did your parents give you that has stuck with you today?

Always be honest. They'd see to it that we'd be that way... or else!

When you arrive in Heaven, who is the first person you want to see?

(Ponders intently for a while) I suppose my mother. Seems like I see her so much now as it is. She was such an influence to me as a child.

Overall, how would you describe your life? Has it been interesting?

Not really. Nothing dramatic ever happened to me. Not one darn thing... nothing unusual. No crises. Never worried about anything. Never thought about worrying.
I've had a really good life. I really don't think I have much of a story to tell. Whatever I wanted, I got. Things just came my way. I got what I desired without worrying if I would get it.
Even when Lloyd and I got our first jobs, we never had to go looking for them. They came to us. We never had to ask. Things were simply given to us.
No big story here. My life has been ordinary. Smooth sailing. No tall tales to tell. I've been lucky.

Extraordinary words from a self-described ordinary woman. A story worthy of sharing with everyone.

No Wonder Grandma's Life Was "Smooth Sailing!"

Back in 1941, Grandma was visiting her sister and nephew in Palm Beach, Florida. This was shortly after World War II began. The British had chased a German ship into Fort Lauderdale Harbor, and when Grandma, her mom, and her sister found out about it, they all dashed down there immediately. The sailors were confined to the ship, but those three ladies stood on the shore and began enthusiastically communicating with them in German. That just made those soldiers' day! Grandma will "koraspond" with anyone, no matter who they are!

DID GRANDMA EXPERIENCE NEW YORK CITY, OR DID NEW YORK CITY EXPERIENCE GRANDMA?

William H. Told, Jr., affectionately known as Billy to the family, was the only child of Grandma's older sister, Sadie, and he has enjoyed a very unique relationship with Grandma over the years and recognizes that Grandma is truly one-of-a-kind.

When Sadie was 21 years old, she left Kansas and headed to Florida, a very bold and ambitious move for a young lady in 1917. Sadie was a huge influence on Grandma, yet uniquely different. She was very sophisticated. She was an accomplished soloist and a music teacher, too. She was, in fact, the supervisor of music for the county of Miami and later became a founding professor of music at the University of Miami around 1930.

Billy recalls the frequent visits Grandma would make to Florida to spend time with Sadie, and he learned a lot about his aunt Kora in those days, as the previous story about the adventures on Coney Island evidenced.

"She was always so well-organized. She had winter clothes, spring clothes, fall clothes, and summer clothes. She had everything organized and lived very efficiently. Her solid work ethic and organizational skills greatly contributed to the success of the pharmacy," noted Billy.

Just as Sadie pushed Billy to become very successful, Billy saw that same drive in his aunt Kora.

"She was very supportive of her two boys. She was their biggest cheerleader. She saw to it that they were trained in music, sports, and academics. She wanted to expand their horizons. She basically laid the groundwork for them, which was very broad-based. She was always very busy in life, but those boys were top drawer to her."

Because of the manner in which Grandma pushed her two boys, they were very successful early on in life. L.A. had an International Rotary Scholarship to England after he graduated from college. Blaine was a Rhodes Scholarship finalist and later won a Fulbright to study in England a couple of years after L.A. had been there. A few years after that, Blaine obtained a Rockefeller Scholarship that took him to Manila in the Philippines.

Evidently, Grandma championed Billy just as much. When he first moved from Palm Beach to New York City in 1955 to assume a job there, Grandma came out right away with my mom and Uncle Blaine. My dad was studying abroad in England, so he missed out on these particular festivities.

"I had just arrived in the city and really didn't know much," noted Billy. "She, however, had the whole city figured out in a heartbeat. She took us to the Stork Club, to the Copa Cabana and to El Morocco. She'd dance and carry on and celebrate with us, paying for it all, to boot! She loved going to the places where "the swells" went...the high society type....she loved to be around celebrities and famous people. I loved it because she was showing me my new city...and I did not even have to pay for the fun! She coordinated the whole experience for us. She was the one who even introduced me to the subway. I don't ordinarily ride it, nor did I want to at the time, but she intended to give me that experience anyway."

Grandma, with all of her bravado and confidence, essentially opened doors for Billy in New York City that he could not possibly imagine. She mastered the Big Apple. She knew what she wanted to see – the elegant night clubs, the performers, and the entertainers. She wanted to enjoy it all, and she most certainly did.

HEAVEN HAS ARRIVED!

When Uncle Blaine was married to his first wife, Kitty, they lived in Houston, Texas. A new bride, admittedly inexperienced in the kitchen, Aunt Kitty knew that my uncle was so accustomed to the sport of eating, and she tried many times to duplicate Grandma's famous recipes in an effort to make my uncle happy. She confesses to encountering defeat on numerous occasions.

"Those Hollinger boys grew up with food at every turn. Food was an event. So many things revolved around food. If you were a Hollinger, you ate. However, I just couldn't cook like Kora," she sighed.

One weekend in the mid-1960s, Grandma and Grandpa made the long drive from Russell to Houston to visit my aunt and uncle. True to form, Grandma cooked an entire Sunday dinner prior to departing and somehow managed to keep the warm parts warm and the cold parts cold for the duration of the drive. We all marvel at how she did it, but she did.

When they pulled up to my uncle's house, Grandma grabbed the dishes from the car and walked to the front door. When my uncle opened the door and saw his mother there, food in her arms, the first thing he said was, "Heaven has arrived!"

GRANDMA HAS ALWAYS HAD A LOVE AFFAIR WITH FOOD AND ADMITS SHE LOVES FOODS THAT ARE FATTENING.

"When I eat, I want to eat!" she declares.

Grandma has always been the consummate hostess and entertainer over the years and would frequently lament with respect to her busy social agenda, "It's terrible!"

YOU CAN ALWAYS FIND A REASON TO GET TOGETHER AND ENJOY GOOD FOOD! THAT'S GRANDPA IN THE MIDDLE OF THE BACK ROW AND GRANDMA, SECOND ON HIS LEFT! MY PARENTS ARE SEATED...DAD IN THE V-NECK SWEATER AND MOM ON HIS LEFT, CIRCA 1958.

AND YOU DON'T HAVE TO BE RELATED TO GRANDMA TO HAVE HER BE YOUR OFFICIAL "MEALS ON WHEELS" KIND OF GAL...

This is an e-mail I received from Jim Barnhill, family friend, currently of Washington State, dated June 30, 2010:

I graduated from Great Bend High, Class of 1949, and met my future wife, Dolores "Dee" McCoy in 1952 on a blind date. We attended several Russell High basketball games with Dee's folks and with the Hollinger family. After the first half, I moved further down the seats, as Kora continually jammed her elbow in my side, shouting, "Did you see that shot?"

Kora played the organ for our wedding on 19 July 1953 at the Congregational Church in Russell. My wife, Dee, class of 1947, was a classmate of Steve Mills and Arlen Specter. Both come back every five years for the class reunion. It has been fun getting to know them.

I commented to Kora early in my marriage that she made the finest baked beans in the world. She remembered that comment. In 1959, we moved to Hillsboro, Texas, where we bought a small daily newspaper with the Townsley family and two men who managed their papers in Russell and Great Bend.

   We were alerted that your grandparents were driving south and would be stopping in Hillsboro to see us. Your grandmother came to the door and delivered a pot of her famous baked beans, baked in her oven 500 miles away in Russell!

   Jim Barnhill

   When in her early 90s, Grandma was asked if she'd be interested in participating in the "Meals on Wheels" program... Her response? "Not now. Don't have time to volunteer!"

DEFINITION OF THE WORD "SLEEP"

Back when Grandma was in elementary school, one of her teachers had her memorize the definition of the word "sleep," that she still recalls to this day, and it goes like this:

"Sleep is that condition of the body in which the normal activity of the nervous system is so far reduced that consciousness is entirely wanting or at an extremely low ebb. "

MANICURES, PEDICURES, AND BLUE HAIR

Grandma has always taken her daily beauty regimen quite seriously. She enjoys weekly manicures, favoring reds and pinks. She appreciates good hair days, too, and a monthly visit to the salon is always in order. We have always joked about her "blue hair" over the years, noting the residue from the dye. When I was a kid, she used to have me take a hair pick and fluff up the hairs on the back of her head to cover the bald spots!

In an effort to keep her hair looking good for up to 30 days, Grandma makes sure to wear a scarf when in the elements and when she sleeps, she rests flat on her back, face towards the ceiling, and she never moves an inch throughout the night. That way, she is guaranteed that her hair will look just as good in the morning as it did the night before.

"I don't get it," she says. "I know people who toss and turn every which way all night long. Not me, boy. I sleep flat on my back with my arms at my side, never moving an inch."

As for her glowing pedicures, it's enough to say that when she lived in Russell, she would make the 30-minute drive to Hays, Kansas every couple of weeks to get her toe nails trimmed. I always thought that was interesting and wondered why someone in her hometown couldn't just do that for her!

GRANDMA'S ANTICIPATED FINAL WORDS

Over the years, Grandma has enjoyed complaining on and off again, in a fun and spirited manner, about her health. Now while she will proudly admit that she has "never been sick a day in her life," there was a period of time…years, perhaps….where she seemed to have a persistent and nagging cough. Nothing too terribly bad. Just a minor cough here and there, and each time she coughed, she would proudly proclaim, "TB!" (As if to suggest she was dying of tuberculosis!)

Still, at 106, she is relatively medicine-free, pain-free, and ailment-free. She used to call upon her two boys for medical advice over the years, but it was usually something that had to do with her bones and joints and things that go "bump" in the body as age sets in. She would call Uncle Blaine and regurgitate her alleged physical complaints. After hearing her out for a few minutes, he would politely tell her, "Now, Mom. You know I can't help you there. I deal with infectious diseases, and L.A., well, he can't help, either. He deals with diseases of the chest. We don't dabble in bones."

When she was 105, Grandma told me that she was contemplating firing her doctor. When I asked her why, she said, "Well, he can't seem to find anything wrong with me. Not a dang thing, and at my age, you SHOULD be able to find something wrong. Can't trust a doctor who can't find anything wrong with me."

Just as she has dutifully attended to every detail of her impending funeral plans (if that even happens!), Grandma has made sure to emphasize that on her tombstone, and she wants the following words inscribed: *"Now won't you believe that I was sick?"*

CLOSING THOUGHTS FOR NEW BEGINNINGS

In retrospect, it would be fascinating to discover what reality is to Kora versus what it is to you and me. I suspect she looks at the world from a completely different perspective than most people do. She has basically wired her brain to believe that all is well and that she has certain things to accomplish and has the unwavering confidence those things will get done. No doubts take up residence in her mind. No negative thinking to interfere. She is not an observer. She is a doer. Perhaps when she looks in the mirror each day, she sees the face of someone from long ago, which has never changed, never aged...just the face of someone who is completing her mission in life and fulfilling her purpose...whatever it takes and for how long it might take. The way I see it, for someone in her 107th year of life and still in the game, I have to think that her express purpose is less for her and more for those whose lives she has touched.

I hope that this does not represent just the end of a book for you, but rather a new beginning as you possibly walk away with at least one word, one phrase, or one idea that sticks with you the remainder of your life. I would like to gently remind you that no matter where you are in life, if you have yet to reach at least 105 years of age, then you have a lot of living yet to do! Get out there and go for it! It's never too late! There is no rule in life that dictates how many chapters a book should have! Make your life story a real page-turner, and if your life ever does flash before your very eyes one day far into the future, make sure it's worth watching!

Love, Ann ☺

FAMILY CRUISE TO MEXICO, JULY 2010
AS GRANDMA SAYS, "MY LIFE HAS ALWAYS BEEN SMOOTH
SAILING"